Advance P

You are in for a treat, dear reader, as Kate writes stunningly of her personal journey from difficulty and heart-break to healing and freedom. She offers here an unflinching account of her life with precision and honesty, directness, and truthfulness. We are engaged from the very first paragraph, and she takes us along on an unsettling yet riveting ride through her discovery of wholeness and health.

This is a timely and much needed book that creates new possibilities for those who have suffered with bipolar disorder without hope. Kate shares her experience that reveals there are alternative pathways, and when combined together in the way she describes in this book, can open a drastically different future. Kate is living proof of the determination and spirit of experimentation and optimism that can create this type of embodied, substantial change.

The ideas contained in this book are not necessarily known or popular, yet they are accessible to those who are sincere in wanting to heal. Kate offers her loving support and advice every step of the way, and offers many, many resources that can lead to reclaiming the life that is our birth right as humans. Her message is clear: you are not alone, and you *can* create a different life of well-being and joy for yourself. This path isn't always easy or simple, yet Kate's description of her process gives us the means and the inspiration to do just that – find ourselves and our wholeness.

– Beatrice W. Hansen

Principal, Presence-Based® Coaching

The modern medical community has largely dismissed the power of the individual to heal many of their own disorders and traumas. In *This Is Me, Bipolar-Free*, Kate gives you all of your power back and reminds you that YOU are in control of your health. Not only does she share her personal journey of trauma and healing but she gives you all the tools you will need to get back on a path toward supreme health and abundance. Read this book, take your power back, and regain your life.

– **Dan Miller**

International Health and Wellness Expert

www.danmiller.tv

As a retired Mental Health Therapist I unfortunately remember informing individuals diagnosed with bi-polar disorder that they would likely have to remain on psychotropic medications for all of their lives. Kate's story of and prescription for hope should be in the toolbox of every mental health therapist. Her book offers a lifestyle guide for healthy living that empowers everyone to take personal control of their lives. I can think of no one that could not benefit from the message of this heartfelt, positive and hopeful book.

– **Larry Weight**

Retired Mental Health Therapist

Kate LaBrosse's courage is reflected on every page of her fascinating self-reflective book. Hers is a fearless testimony of how ownership of one's own power heals from within. As her very personal story attests, ultimately it's hard work and trust in one's self that brings freedom, health, and joy.

– **JOHN STONE**

Retired, Former CEO of The Children's Neurology Foundation

Kate LaBrosse's book, *This Is Me, Bipolar-Free: Heal Your Mental Illness and Create Your Authentic Life,* is an amazing guidebook for those looking to naturally heal their mental illness. This book specifically addresses those diagnosed with bipolar disorder but could most certainly be used as a guide to heal other mental illnesses such as depression or anxiety.

The author uses her experience with bipolar II disorder, childhood trauma and depression, her ICF Presence Based coaching training, and her expert knowledge of the natural products industry to guide readers through the method she created to naturally heal her own bipolar disorder. She outlines an approach that addresses the whole person – the body, mind, and soul – and shares the very detailed and extensive process that it takes to heal yourself. She does an incredible job of breaking down each step within the twelve chapters of the book, making the readers' desired outcome feel obtainable.

Throughout the book she is raw and honest, sharing her life's journey living with bipolar, which makes her relatable to the reader. She explains that looking within yourself and doing the work it takes to heal your mental illness is not always easy; it is a process and it takes time and dedication. However, persistence will allow noticeable changes to show up in the readers' life. Although taking the first step and subsequent steps may feel daunting, she is right there with the reader every step of the way, cheering them on and encouraging them to keep going because the end result is worth the effort. Her program empowers the reader to successfully take the steps in the program to truly heal themselves and set them free from their mental illness, so they can begin living a life they love!

– **Kristy Conlan**
Beyond Quantum
Website: www.kristyconlan.com
Facebook: www.facebook.com/BeyondQuantumOfficial
Instagram: @beyondquantumofficial

Kate LaBrosse describes an easily implemented and compassionate guide to change, from the nuts and bolts to the deeply transformative. This is a book that will be valuable for anyone to read and use – but especially for those with a bipolar disorder diagnosis.

– **Joel Ronningen**
Myofascial Therapist and Qigong Instructor
Ametrine Bodyworks
http://www.ametrinebodyworks.com/

With a strong determination to help others heal their mental illness naturally, Kate LaBrosse offers up holistic approaches and scientific facts to back them up.

Kate lays out a plan that is practical for those struggling with mental illness and even for those who are just looking for more balance in their lives. In seven steps, she shows how adjusting your diet, taking time for meditation, body movement and exercise, plus permitting yourself to do the work, can lead to sustainable healing.

Kate's story of not only surviving but thriving after living with a mental illness is an inspiration for anyone who has lived with bipolar disorder or any other mental disorder. Not only is her story inspirational, but it's a testament to the healing path discussed in her book.

I am confident that you will find a practice in *This Is Me, Bipolar-Free* that will lead you onto a path of balance and healing.

– **Charles Minguez**
Writer and Mental Health Advocate
Twitter: https://twitter.com/CharlesMinguez

Kate's dedication to her own healing process is impressive. I could feel a mix of vulnerability, power, and authenticity in her story. She passionately shares transformative tools for naturally healing a bipolar diagnosis. *This Is Me, Bipolar-Free* is a practical, comprehensive guide to living your best life through diet, mindfulness, and self-care. The holistic toolkit she outlines is a wonderful reference for those who are bipolar and beyond!

– **Kaitlynn Minguez**
Reiki Master

Do not skip the Author's Note! Kate LaBrosse starts right out of the gate by asking you the big questions, calling out the deeper truths, and establishing realizable potentials. The greatest gift of this book is that you come to know that bipolar CAN be overcome because Kate has done it! She provides you with a step-by-step process towards healing mentally, physically, emotionally, and spiritually, all the aspects of bipolar, using a full-system holistic approach. *This Is Me, Bipolar-Free* provides the reader with a wealth of information, tools, science, and practices as Kate weaves her own story and wisdom throughout the book. The message is, you *can* move beyond bipolar through desire, focus, persistence, consistency, and many times down right hard work. But, it is possible and you, the reader, are left knowing that healing is possible and that there is a path forward.

– **Jeanne Lecher**

Communication Specialist and Energy Consultant

https://www.jeannelecher.com/

You do not have to be bipolar to benefit from Kate's wisdom. Coming from the heart of a woman who has done the work to heal herself, Kate's 7 steps clearly articulate a process for you to create space to heal whatever is causing you dis-ease in your life. Through a gentle weaving of her recovery story with an extensive variety of options available for you to explore, Kate masterfully guides you to develop your own roadmap through the healing process. While addressing the physical, emotional, and spiritual aspects of the healing process, Kate also provides a pre-view of the joy, gratitude, and peace that can accompany you along your journey of self-healing.

– **Laura Strong**

Founder of The Metamorphosis Center

Wow! This book is amazing. Kate LaBrosse is not only candid, down to earth and open about the abuse and bipolar disorder that once consumed her life, but her heart wrenching story leads you through the many discoveries she made along the way to help her heal. In this book, Kate openly shares her journey from abuse to bipolar to freedom.

When the medical and pharmaceutical systems failed her another suicide attempt brought her to rock bottom, where she somehow finds the courage to start listening to what her body had been trying to tell her all along. As she follows her internal guidance, she begins to explore nutrition, vitamins, supplements, exercise, meditation, breath work and energy healing and is eventually able to gently unwind the trauma her body had been holding.

Through the lens of experience, Kate is now able to guide you in a step by step process that worked for her and can work for you too. This book is not only for those with bipolar disorder or someone with mental illness, it is for anyone that wants to clear trauma out of their bodies and lead a more positive, rewarding and joy-filled life.

Kate clearly and thoughtfully explains the many approaches, tips and tools that are out there and weaves together a plethora of cutting edge, well-researched, holistic practices that anyone can follow and implement. And she holds your hand along the way. She is gentle, compassionate and supportive as she reminds you that if she can do it, anyone can. This book will change your life.

– TERRI PETERSON

Nationally Recognized Breathwork Facilitator

www.theconnectingspirit.com

This is Me, Bipolar Free

THIS IS *Me,* BIPOLAR-FREE

Heal Your Mental Illness & Create Your Authentic Life

KATE LABROSSE

NEW YORK

LONDON • NASHVILLE • MELBOURNE • VANCOUVER

This is Me, Bipolar Free

Heal Your Mental Illness and Create Your Authentic Life

Published in New York, New York, by Morgan James Publishing in partnership with Difference Press. Morgan James is a trademark of Morgan James, LLC.
www.MorganJamesPublishing.com

ISBN 9781642794229 paperback
ISBN 9781642794236 eBook
ISBN 9781642795301 audio
Library of Congress Control Number: 2018968037

Cover Design by:
Christopher Kirk
www.GFSstudio.com

Interior Design by:
Chris Treccani
www.3dogcreative.net

For my tribe. My soul family who have always seen me as whole and healthy. You held the space for my authentic life to emerge when I was too tired, afraid, or lost to hold it for myself.

And to all beings who are doing the brave, deep work of healing themselves. This world needs you and I bow to you.

Table of Contents

Author's Note

Get ready, this book is going to challenge everything you have been taught about your bipolar disorder and our entire mental "health" industry. I'm going to ask you to stay open and curious while you read this book. Start by asking yourself, "What if?" What if it's truly possible to heal your mental illness? What if your medications are doing more harm than good? What if food really does have the power to heal? What if everything that you've been through has actually served a divine purpose? What if your rollercoaster emotions aren't out to get you but are designed to be your compass? What if by facing your traumas you free yourself from them forever? What if you stop believing that your mind is in charge and that your thoughts are truth? What if, by changing your mindset, you change the course of your life forever? What if you remember that you're a soul having a human experience and that your body is not a prison but is in fact designed to be your partner? What if you're more powerful than you truly know, and your own power has the ability to heal you completely?

These are big questions, I know. But you're here for a reason – you are reading this book for a reason. And that reason is that on some level, you already know the truth. You know that your life is not meant to be lived in a state of disease. You know that you're being called to find a way to effectively manage and ultimately heal your disorder so that you can then shift your energy toward creating a life that feels authentically yours. You know that you are meant for something more – and you know that you'll never be able to actualize the future life that is calling out to you if you don't heal your mental illness.

Stay open and curious as you read this book. Allow room for the unknown and the unexperienced. Keep your mind in a state of curiosity and "what if-ness" so that you can fully receive the information laid out in this book. It's okay to maintain your skepticism. It's okay to do "gut checks" along the way to see what truly resonates for you. It's okay to do fact checks along the way, too. A lot of what I'm about to share with you is based on my own personal experience and the program that I've created to help others heal. However, the viability of these methodologies, treatments, and lifestyle changes has ample scientific research and case studies to back it up – feel free to do research on your own. Be wary though because the most widely held belief about bipolar disorder is still that it's not something that can be healed – it's something that you will have to manage for the rest of your life. I am here as living proof that that is 100% false. So be discerning in what you choose to put your attention on and belief in because if your intent is to disprove what I teach in this book you'll do it and, true healing will only happen if you start to believe that it can.

This book is constructed around holistic, or full-system, healing. To me, your 'system' is the totality of who you truly [illegible] mental, emotional, physical, and energetic bodies. It is the partnership between your body and your spirit. It is your physical and your vibrational makeup. This book is grounded in the fact that all pieces of your system need to be brought back into a state of balance and vitality in order to fully heal *and* that you cannot address one issue in one area of the body without taking into account every other area. Every piece of us is intimately interconnected and healing your bipolar disorder will ultimately mean healing your entire system.

I am so happy that you're here. Truly. This book was written for you, the person who has persevered to get to this point. The person who is ready for something more, something greater and something deeper. I say it in my dedication and I'll say it again, I bow to you. Doing healing work is brave – you are brave. My purpose, my greater life that was calling to me during my healing process is here now. I am living my purpose by helping others see their truths, deeply heal themselves, and harness their own power. So, as you read this, know that above all else, I am here, holding the possibility and the space for you to truly heal – because I know that that's the truth of who you are.

Chapter 1

Brave Warrior, You Have Been Forged in the Fire

"Some days, I feel everything at once. Other days, I feel nothing at all. I don't know what's worse – drowning beneath the waves or dying from the thirst."

– ANONYMOUS

The American Psychiatric Association defines bipolar disorder in this way: "Bipolar disorders are brain disorders that cause changes in a person's mood, energy and ability to function. Bipolar disorder is a category that includes three different conditions – bipolar I, bipolar II and cyclothymic disorder. People with bipolar disorders have extreme and intense emotional states that occur at distinct times, called mood episodes. These mood episodes are categorized as manic, hypomanic or depressive."

What a benign way to define something that is an all-consuming, life-altering, crazy-making, rollercoaster way of living. Or maybe more appropriately put, a way of *existing*, because when you're in the throes of this mental illness you're not really living – you're hanging on for dear life, doing what you can do just to stay stable and sane. To try and keep your mind from telling your body to take a swan dive off the tallest cliff you can find or to not walk out the door and keep walking with the hope of disappearing forever.

This illness robs you of everything. Your ability to genuinely connect with others – your family, your friends, your coworkers, your significant other. It robs you of your will to live. It robs you of your ability to discern what's in your best interest and talks you into doing things that could literally kill you. It causes you to question every single emotion you have and even worse, to begin to fear the positive feelings because – what if they aren't real – just the beginning of another manic episode? It makes it so you're unable to get out of bed for weeks at a time, but can't actually sleep, despite being utterly exhausted. But then, it can push you to stay up for days in a state of euphoria with seemingly unending energy that is both amazing and terrifying because somewhere inside of you, you know that it's self-destructive and ultimately, you have no control over it.

The swings can be subtler, too. They don't have to be the super high highs or the super low lows – although in my experience the lows were almost always super low or usually for me, deadly low. These subtler swings are pervasive and begin to infiltrate your being so completely that you stop recognizing them as the disorder and begin to identify yourself *as* them. You start to lose the ability to see where the disorder starts and you begin. You begin to believe that you are someone who can't make up their mind, who is afraid of everything, who gets panicked even thinking about starting something new, who falls in and out of love without any effort, who leaves a trail of brokenness in their wake, who is unable to coexist with others, and who will always, at least to some extent, be a burden to those around you.

There is also the flip side to this too – a side that's almost entitled and defiant. Our diagnosis gives us the reason to be able to say to others:

- "Sorry, not sorry. It's not me who did that thing that hurt you, it's my disorder."
- "I can't help you with that project … go to that meeting … follow through on what I committed to … because I'm in the middle of an episode."
- "You have to help me … save me … take responsibility for me because my bipolar doesn't allow me to do those things for myself."

Our disorder becomes our 'get out of jail free card.' And it works for a while – until the people in our lives begin losing their patience with us and start saying:

- "Enough is enough."
- "I love you, but I can't be around this anymore."
- "I can't be your punching bag anymore."
- "I can't watch you hurt yourself anymore."

- "There is nothing in this world, including your illness, that justifies what you did to me."

Until one day you look around and realize that the people who love you have all put up boundaries to protect themselves from … YOU. This realization washes over you in ways that steal the last bits of yourself that you still felt good about. It takes the last shards of hope you had and shatters them completely.

And then the guilt and shame set in. You see how alone you are and you both resent your friends and family for abandoning you and hate yourself for being, doing, and saying the things you did that hurt them enough to make them walk away from you. This reinforces your deep-seated belief that you really are worthless and unlovable and not deserving of anything good in your life. Marya Hornbacher says it perfectly in her book, *Madness: A Bipolar Life*, "Soon madness has worn you down. It's easier to do what it says than argue. In this way, it takes over your mind. You no longer know where it ends and you begin. You believe anything it says. You do what it tells you, no matter how extreme or absurd. If it says you're worthless, you agree. You plead for it to stop. You promise to behave. You are on your knees before it, and it laughs."

You look around and you wonder, "How in the world did I end up here?" and you remember back to when you first got diagnosed and how relieved you were. People who haven't been where you've been will never fully be able to comprehend how you were able to feel gratitude and the overwhelming sense of comfort and hope that came when your doctor gave you this diagnosis. I remember when I got diagnosed – I was 25 and getting that diagnosis felt like

I had finally been given the meaning of life – or at least my life. It explained my "crazy," gave me context for understanding why I was the way I was, and filled me with so much hope because I would finally be able to take a pill and begin a treatment that would help me. And, I could maybe stop feeling like I wanted to end it all on a daily basis.

For most of us who receive this diagnosis, we have already suffered so much and have lived in fear, isolation, and confusion for so long that the diagnosis itself becomes our lifeline. For most of us, by the time we get our diagnosis we have already hurt ourselves, lost control, put ourselves in debilitating debt, abused our bodies, ruined relationships, convinced ourselves that we're crazy, and in extreme cases – attempted suicide. We may have previously been diagnosed with depression or suffered from panic attacks. We may have been prescribed antidepressants and spent time and money on therapy. All these things just further solidified our belief that we truly must be crazy because medication and therapy weren't working.

So then, when the day comes that the doctor gives you your diagnosis – it feels like a gift and the answer to your prayers. Because now you have something to help you and those who love you understand and because there's now a bit of hope that relief will be possible.

You then throw yourself into figuring out your newfound reality. You read books and blogs, listen to podcasts, join support groups, take every medication that your doctors prescribe you – including the ones for sleep, the ones to stabilize your moods, and the ones to keep your panic at bay. You start keeping track of your moods and your sleep cycle. You become hyper-vigilant about any perceived shift in your state of being so that you can recognize the onset of an episode. You enlist others to monitor you too because you now know that you're not fully capable of recognizing your own behaviors. You start to wear your diagnosis like a badge of honor. You tell anyone who will listen, "I have bipolar" because you just know that if they are aware of your illness, they'll understand you better, make allowances for you, and treat you with care. Above all else, they'll understand just how special you truly are – because your diagnosis sets you apart from the crowd.

And don't let anyone tell you otherwise, there is something almost magical about being bipolar. You're able to feel things that most others can't. You experience transcendent passion and creativity. You begin to love your manic episodes because they unleash a power within you. David Lovelace describes it like this in his book, *Scattershot: My Bipolar Family*, "Compared to bipolar's magic, reality seems a raw deal." And he's right – the thought of having to be normal seems tedious and boring. There is a part of us that doesn't want to truly heal for fear of losing the magic of our mania.

But at some point, maybe after your doctor changed your medications – again – or after you lost yet another job, broke a relationship so badly it's not fixable, filed bankruptcy, got diagnosed with a STD, disappeared from your life and made your friends and family fear that you were dead, or found yourself in a hospital, getting your stomach pumped after an overdose – you realized that this disorder is not the blessing you thought it was. That it is truly a living nightmare. That the traditional therapies and medications that were supposed to keep you sane, safe, and balanced and maybe even happy are probably, at worst, doing the exact opposite of what they're designed to do or at best, have numbed you and made you into a muted version of yourself.

And then you feel lost all over again. But now you're angry and confused too because you followed the direction of your doctor and talked about your childhood traumas with a therapist and took all the meds you were prescribed – you have been such a good little bipolar patient – but none of it worked. Not really. You might be slightly more stable, or maybe even a lot more stable - but sort of operate in a state of numbness. Or you could be a whole lot less stable. But one thing is for sure – you're not healthy. You still don't feel good most of the time. You live your life on constant high alert, looking for the next episode to strike. And worst of all – your life is not your own. It's still being run by this disease.

What I want you to know is that whatever brought you to this point, whatever your story is, whether you wore your diagnosis loud and proud or locked it away because of embarrassment and shame, whatever you've had to endure to bring you to this day is exactly what needed to happen. And – above all else – you are a warrior. Because battling this disorder, constantly battling yourself, and battling your own mind while protecting yourself from the prejudices and stereotypes of mental illness, is one of the hardest things that anyone could possibly have to do. So, the fact that you're still standing, still striving to figure this thing out, here today, reading this book, continuing to look for answers, makes you the ultimate warrior. I am in awe of you.

There is a piece of you, the piece of you that's greater than your disorder, that's greater than your pain, that's greater than your shame, that's greater than all the hurt you've amassed, that is more powerful than your broken brain, broken body, and broken heart, that is calling out and asking you to find a better way. This piece of you, whatever you call it … your soul, spirit, or higher-self, is asking you to create a life of joy, purpose, passion, meaning, creativity, and love. It is pointing you in the direction of your own true path – one that is not defined, in any way, by the diagnosis of bipolar disorder, depression or anxiety.

Healing is not a miracle, it is the coming together of right thoughts and right actions and is corroborated by spiritual principles and scientific facts. I will teach you the steps I took to heal my own bipolar disorder. Steps that, at the time, were foreign to me, but that emerging neuroscience now validates. I will show you how I was able to balance my emotional, physical, mental, and spiritual bodies and ultimately create a life that is authentically mine, one that I am proud of and in love with.

Take the steps seriously. This work isn't for the weak-willed. But you're anything but weak – you've survived the prison that is bipolar and you are on your own hero's journey. I am so grateful to be here to support you as you come to fully believe what I know to be true: you are not your diagnosis, you are not what happened to you or what has been put upon you. You are not the mistakes you've made or the people you've hurt. You are worthy of a beautiful life. You are the creator of your own story and you have the power inside of you to write yourself a fairytale and create a life that lights you up.

"What you seek is seeking you."

– RUMI

Chapter 2

Finding A Way Through and Lighting the Way To

"When desperation and willingness meet,
miracles can happen."
– Dr. Christiane Northrop

Have you ever wanted to just walk out of your life and disappear? More than just disappear – cease being altogether? There was a time in my life where there was nothing that I wanted more than that. It wasn't about wanting to kill myself – although I attempted that several times – it was about just wanting to be gone – to be freed from the torturous prison of my own body, emotions, and mind. My resounding thought for years was "I want to go home." This was what I would sob, over and over again when I was in my depressive episodes. "I want to go home, I want to go home, I want to go home …." To me, it was Home with a capital H. I wanted my soul to be at peace. I wanted to go back to where we come from. I longed for the peace, all-knowingness, and unconditional love that is promised to us when we're on the other side, not in physical form. Home was my word for Heaven and living in my own personal Hell made me crave it with every fiber of my being.

So, that is exactly what I did, on February 12th, 2009 I walked out of my life with the intent of going Home. I was 29 years old and owned a dog daycare facility with my mom. I was at work with our groomer and told her that I had to go to the bank and would be right back. I walked out on my responsibilities to my mom that day, my responsibilities to my employees and my responsibilities to our customers – and never went back. I didn't know where I was going when I walked out. I started driving, having one of the worst panic attacks of my life – and I ended up in an unfamiliar city. I wasn't sure what to do next, but a plan was beginning to form. I went to a mall – a mall of all places! And I bought things that I felt would bring me comfort – slippers, a neck wrap, pajamas, and bath salts. I then booked a hotel room – one with a fireplace and a jacuzzi – because my driving desire was – for one moment, just one solitary moment, I wanted to feel comfort and love and peace. Then I filled my lorazepam prescription. I did all this as preparation for ending my life.

I obviously didn't succeed in ending my life that night. Through a series of divine events my friends and family found me at that hotel. And my ex-boyfriend, Josh, who was literally one of my guardian angels and whom I credit for me still being alive today, stayed with me at the hotel that night and supported me fully over the next several months as I let my life fall completely apart so that I could begin the process of creating one that I actually wanted to live.

My life up until that point was filled with one trauma, devastation, and heartbreak after another that started in my mom's womb. Through regression therapy, I was able to access a memory of my dad violently shaking and threatening my mom while she was pregnant with me. This was the first of many physical traumas I would face in my life. And the first of many emotional traumas, too. During my session I could hear my mom sobbing and feel fear coursing through her body and my own. My dad is an alcoholic who also abused drugs and is most likely dealing with his own undiagnosed bipolar disorder. My dad – who was really only ever a dad in title only – made it very clear to me throughout my childhood, adolescence, and young adult years that I was unwanted, unworthy, and undeserving of his love – or anyone else's. These beliefs were hardwired into my system and the process of unearthing, transforming, healing, and releasing them has been one of the greatest challenges greatest gifts of my life.

My next great trauma was being sexually abused by my stepdad. Steve came into my life when I was around a year old and for a while I know it was good. I was happy and so was my mom. But a switch was flipped in Steve when my mom got pregnant with my brother. I don't know all the reasons why this triggered him, but I do know that it was something that terrified him and that was when the abuse started.

The abuse continued for several years until it eventually transferred to my brother. Neither my brother nor I had conscious memories of the abuse for most of our lives. My memories didn't surface until I had gotten far enough along in my healing journey and I was able to handle them. I was 30 when the first memories came back to me. I kept these memories to myself for a long time because I had no idea how to make any sense of them, I wasn't ready to fully face them, and because Steve was still very much involved in my life, my brother's life, and the lives of our family members. Despite the abuse, Steve had just been my dad up until that point. He wasn't necessarily a present dad, but he provided for us and I knew he loved us. When I finally started to separate myself from Steve it began a chain reaction that changed the course of our family forever. My reclaimed memories also opened up the space for my brother's memories to start coming back to him and ultimately led us to estrange ourselves from Steve completely. The full story is too much to share here, but it does have a beautiful ending. Through a lot of individual therapy and healing work, my brother and I got to a place where we began family therapy with Steve and we were able to do deep healing, reconnect, and forgive before Steve passed away just this year, one day after his 66th birthday.

Sexual abuse and violence continued to be a pattern in my life – two of my cousins and I were sexually abused by a step uncle when I was 7. I was then drugged and raped during a party when I was 21. I also had many "smaller" instances of sexual violation throughout my life, including being stalked by a neighborhood flasher when I was a kid and, like all too many women, had to fend off inappropriate behavior from friends, family, and colleagues. My body became an unsafe place to be and the only way I could survive it was to almost completely disconnect from it.

Despite all these abuses though, I led a fairly normal, healthy, productive life. It wasn't until I was 23 and started the dog business with my mom that things imploded. I became severely depressed, anxious, and began having panic attacks. I started seeing a therapist and was diagnosed with depression and prescribed antidepressants. I was also given medications to help me sleep and to fend off the panic. It was during this time that I attempted suicide for the first time. This attempt was a textbook "cry for help," but unfortunately true help was still many years away.

I was finally diagnosed with Bipolar II when I was 25 and, like I described in the previous chapter, felt hope for the first time in years. I threw myself into my diagnosis. I wanted to know everything I could about it. For a time, things got a little better. I was put on all new medications, began to incorporate some safeguards, and worked with my therapist to develop disorder management techniques. I wanted my family to understand my disorder too, so I had the whole crew – my mom, brother, grandma, aunts, uncles, and cousins – come to my psychiatrist's office one evening so he could explain this disorder to them. I joined a support group. I read books. I became a walking, talking, self-proclaimed bipolar expert.

But then things got worse – even worse than they were before. So, my doctor changed my meds, and for the next several years my medications were changed and tweaked so many times that I couldn't even tell you now the names of everything I was on. I attempted suicide again. I alienated friends and family. I exhausted myself with my own 'craziness' – not to mention exhausting everyone else around me. I had so much rage bubbling up in me and no outlet to release it appropriately, so it just started pouring out onto anyone who was in a five-mile radius. I amassed mountains of debt. I started and stopped a million projects and left chaos in my wake. I checked myself into the psychiatric ward at a hospital for fear of attempting suicide a third time. I got to a point where I distrusted everyone and everything – most of all myself. I was trapped in a state of pure torture and I saw no way out.

… Except to walk out of my life and disappear forever.

Which brings us back to the day I walked out on my business and on my life. This day ended up being the first day of the rest of my life – although I didn't know it at the time. This was the day I made a promise to myself, the ultimate promise, a promise that has led me to this very place. The promise was this: *"If I'm going to stay here, on this planet, living this life, in this body, then I am going to find a way to truly heal."* I knew somewhere inside of me that I wasn't meant to live in a state of pain and disease. That *none* of us are meant to live in that awful state, where it feels like your own body, brain, and emotions are attacking you. This belief has proven itself to be true not only in my life but in the lives of so many others. It can be true for you too.

As I said earlier, I never went back to the dog daycare. The stress of running a business – more specifically, running a business with my mom – was more than I could physically or emotionally handle. So I quit. Which did nothing but make me feel even more like an absolute and utter failure. But, there was just enough of a pinprick of light that opened up inside of me by making this choice that I stuck with it. I latched onto that bit of light with everything I had. And I kept repeating my promise to myself.

I had no idea how to find true healing and conventional medicine was of absolutely no help. I'll never forget the day I asked my psychiatrist about fish oil. I had never taken fish oil before, I had never heard of it before, but it kept popping up in the research I was doing on treating bipolar disorder naturally. So, I printed off everything I could find and brought it to my doctor, sat across the desk from him, slid the papers toward him with the hope that he would help me understand and strategize. His response was to slide the papers back across the desk to me and say, "I don't know anything about this, I can't help you." It was at that moment that I knew this was going to be a battle I would have to fight on my own. My doctor was not a partner in my healthcare – he was only ever going to be someone that would work with me on "sickness-care."

I continued to do research and found a company called True Hope. They are based in Canada and offer natural supplements for treating mental illness, mainly bipolar disorder. They talked on their website about the possibility of being medication-free! This was the miracle I had been searching for and it filled me with hope! Except I couldn't afford it, my lack of a job and financial mess did not allow for me to spend money every month on supplements that I didn't even know would work. But Josh, that guardian angel that I mentioned before, found a way and ordered my first month's supply. I took two different capsules – one was called Empower Plus, which was the actual vitamin and mineral designed to support a bipolar brain. The second was a probiotic – because according to them, it didn't matter what else you took if your gut wasn't in proper working order and able to digest and assimilate the other supplements you were taking. Mind blown. You have to remember, this was almost ten years ago and probiotics were not the buzzword they are today. I had never heard of them! They made absolutely no sense to me. Neither did the Empower Plus supplement but I took them both religiously.

And, you know where this is going – I started feeling better. Over the course of the next six months I was able to gradually increase my Empower Plus dosage and decrease my medication dosages, until the day came that I was officially medication-free. I still have the email from True Hope that says, "Congratulations, You're Medication-Free!" Almost ten years later, I am still free from the shackles of medications. There have been no more suicide attempts. No more hospitalizations. No more panic attacks. No more bipolar episodes. This is something I am immensely proud of and grateful for.

I no longer take supplements from True Hope – but that is only because I have incorporated so many other healthy habits into my life that I don't need them any longer.

Once I started feeling sane I could shift my energy and attention to whole-life healing, not just bipolar management. I applied for and got a job managing a wellness department at a local health food store. I knew next to nothing about the natural products industry – only that a probiotic and some vitamins and minerals had helped save my life – but, by some miracle, I got that job and it changed my life forever. I still work in the industry and through it I have unearthed the truth of who I really am and have created a life that is greater than anything I could have ever imagined. I have amassed immeasurable knowledge about the industry of food, GMOs, organics, vitamins, minerals, supplements, homeopathics, parabens, sulfates, and synthetic fragrances. You'll find more information on these topics throughout the book and will come to learn how you can support your body's healing abilities through proper diet and supplementation and the elimination of toxins.

In addition to diet changes, I also began incorporating stress-reduction techniques, body work, somatic exercises, yoga, breath work, shamanic work, spiritual practices, affirmations, and visualizations. Each new experience, skill, or level of knowledge opened up something deeper in me and created more abundance, love, and joy. I won't go so far as to say I've tried every healing modality out there, but I have tried more than I can count – and they run the gamut from the conventional westernized systems to ancient Eastern traditions to the ultra "woo-woo" spiritual and energetic practices.

I took all these steps without knowing what I was doing – there was a lot of trial and error, experimentation, and quite a few detours. My hope in writing this book is that I can take some of the guesswork out of your own healing journey and provide you with a roadmap to your own authentic state of health. I will outline for you the steps I took to heal my bipolar disorder and ultimately become the conscious, deliberate creator of my own life.

I have learned so much throughout my journey but the three greatest lessons I've learned, that have now become My Deep Truths and are fully incorporated into who and what I am, are:

- I am grateful for everything. All of it. I would not be the person I am today without the sum of all my experiences and I deeply love who I am today.

- It is never done. There is always another layer of healing. Another lesson to learn. Another path to take. And that this process is beautiful and messy and sometimes painful but always divinely perfect. And it's the reason we're here.
- We are more powerful than we know. Like superhero powerful. We are magic so therefore we have the ability to create magic. And, the time is now to tap into our super powers so that we can heal ourselves, help heal others and the planet, and ultimately become the unstoppable creators we were born to be!

Healing your bipolar disorder is just the beginning; what is possible for you, from a healed state, is more than you can probably imagine from where you're sitting today. So, start on your own healing path then go create magic. Become who you were meant to be. Heal your beautiful broken heart. Create a life of meaning. Own your power and your greatness. I'm here to support and guide you – use my story as proof that healing is possible. You've got this.

"Maybe the reason we tell our stories is so that other women will see that they are allowed to change – and hopefully they won't have to almost die before they give themselves that permission. Maybe if enough of us share our brave stories of transformation and truth, then not so many of us will have to come to the brink of total annihilation before we say 'Enough.'"

– ELIZABETH GILBERT

Chapter 3

From Fighting to Overcome to Choosing to Become

"A miracle that's possible for anyone
is possible for EVERYONE."
– Gregg Braden

Healing my bipolar wasn't actually a miracle – it's the result of holding firmly to my belief that life was not meant to be lived in a state of illness, keeping my promise to myself to find a way to true health, following the guidance that was given to me, taking right action, being willing to be present with my pain, getting comfortable with vulnerability, and making my vision for my own authentic life more important than anything else. This is how I manifested the miraculous, and, this is why I can say with 100% certainty that the "miracle" I experienced is absolutely possible for you to experience as well. I've walked the path and have proven what's possible – so that now, there are steps for you to follow. In the coming chapters I lay out the path I took and the methods I use in my program, as a step-by-step process. Follow them and find your miracle.

- Step 1 – Heal your body, through diet, supplementation and the elimination of toxins
- Step 2 – Get balanced by using sleep, meditation, and movement (plus a few other suggestions)
- Step 3 – Heal and release the traumas trapped in your body through somatic practices
- Step 4 – Learn to listen to and understand the guidance that your body and emotions are always giving you
- Step 5 – Unearth your joy and see why creating joy is an actual step in the healing process and not the end result
- Step 6 – Find your tribe – you're not meant to do this alone
- Step 7 – Become the conscious and deliberate creator of your own life by developing a state of gratitude, getting clear on your vision and purpose, and harnessing the power of affirmations and visualizations

I encourage you to read the book through to the end once, then go back and read one chapter at a time so that you can begin incorporating these changes into your life and create a new way of being. Steps 3–7 can be done concurrently and out of order if that's what resonates for you, but you should not attempt to tackle any of these steps until you have implemented and firmly incorporated Steps 1 and 2. Step 1 is the foundation for everything and Step 2 will create a state of balance; without following through on Steps 1 and 2 before moving on you will not have the base you need for the others to be effective.

Step 1 is all about healing the physical – your brain and your body. I'll explain the gut-brain connection, clarify how the typical American diet is literally causing inflammation and disfunction in your brain, and will walk you through recommended diet changes that will create the platform for real healing and transformation to occur. We'll look at recommended supplements, including vitamins, minerals, herbs, and probiotics that are designed to heal inflammation, balance hormones, restore stability, and create vitality. You'll also see how what you're putting on your body and using to clean your house can make you sick, how to reduce the number of toxins that you're exposed to by changing your household and personal care products, why this matters, and how it correlates to mental health. There will be a lot of information in this chapter. Take it one piece at a time and do what you can. For some, you may already be doing a few of the things that I describe; for others, this will be your first exposure to a brand-new way of eating and consuming. Again, do what you can. The most important piece will be to eliminate harmful food triggers and to heal the gut, so focus on those pieces and incorporate the rest as you can. I'll walk you through all of this.

Step 2 is all about bringing a natural rhythm and balance back to the body. We'll explore how to do this through somatic practices, breath work, meditation, stress reduction, physical activity, mindfulness techniques, light therapy, and quality sleep. I'll provide many different options, so you can experiment and find the ones that best support your body.

In Step 3 we'll look at how to heal your broken heart. As we've already talked about, bipolar disorder leaves a trail of brokenness in its wake. I know that you did not get to this point without having experienced trauma or having created trauma. We'll talk about talk therapy – and how it has its place but how real healing can happen when you release the trapped emotions and traumas that your body is holding onto.

As someone with bipolar disorder your emotions have probably felt more like your enemies than your allies; Step 4 will show you that that couldn't be further from the truth. You'll see that your emotions truly are your compass and your body is your partner on this wild ride. They have their own innate intelligence and together, they are always pointing you toward your own true path. Emotions are the navigation system that our bodies use to communicate with us and when you learn how to understand the signals you'll never be steered off course again.

Step 5 is where we bring in the fun! But, if your story is anything like mine, you may be so far off course from a life that feels amazing that you don't really remember what fun is. You have forgotten how to play. You haven't felt true, free-flowing joy in a very long time, if ever. You've shut down the feelings of passion and the energy of creativity. We're going to identify ways that you can open these spaces back up so that you can see what this new, amazing life that you're creating for yourself might actually look and feel like.

Step 6 is all about your tribe. Finding it, building it, keeping it. We'll talk about why you absolutely need to build relationships with people who are able to see you as whole and healed. And, we'll talk about how your existing relationships will almost certainly change or fall away altogether as you begin this transformative process.

In Step 7 we'll explore how emerging neuroscience now corroborates what spiritual practitioners have known forever – that our thoughts, beliefs, emotions, and energetic vibration really do create our realities. I'll walk you through the heart-brain connection and show you how to use affirmations, visualizations, and the Law of Attraction to align yourself to the life you want and how to design a life that is filled with meaning, joy, passion, love, and abundance … and anything else that lights you up!

But … and this is a BIG BUT … before you do any of this, before you read the next chapters, before you take any of the steps, the first thing that needs to happen is you need to create a belief system around this truth:

You have the power to fully heal yourself. You have everything needed to create a world for yourself where you are not mentally ill. You are meant to be healthy. True healing is truly possible and it's yours for the creating.

I encourage you to put the above into an "I" statement … "I have the power to fully heal myself. I have everything needed …" and write it down, put it someplace that you'll see multiple times throughout the day. Spend time with it, use it as an affirmation. Repeat it to yourself over and over again until it starts to feel true for you. Look at it when you first get up in the morning and again right before you go to sleep, set a timer on your phone so that you stop throughout the day and repeat it ten times. It doesn't need to resonate fully for you before you move on – but there should be some spark that you connect with before taking the next step. Building this belief in your system will get your mind and body on board and will align yourself to a future you that is free from bipolar. This action will harness the power of the Law of Attraction, which we'll go into further, later in the book.

This is not just some spiritual, woo-woo philosophy. There is science to back this up. Scientists, teachers and authors like Bruce Lipton, Dr. Joe Dispenza, Gregg Braden, and Dawson Church all teach some version of this fundamental truth: you have the ability to change your genes, to retrain your brain, to create a reality you want by putting yourself in alignment with that future, TODAY … even though it's not true, YET, even though you don't feel it, YET, even though your doctor or your spouse or your mom is telling you something different. Even though someone with a degree says it isn't possible, even though there is still a part of you that is skeptical, or feels hopeless … do it anyway, speak the words, see yourself as healthy, begin to imagine what that future version of you looks, feels, talks, and acts like. Imagine what you do with your day when it isn't filled with fear, shame, and isolation. Begin to imagine a future where you actually want to be in your body. Where you are grateful for your life. Where you are filled with a sense of love and wonder and optimism.

And do this every day. Make room for this in your life – because make no mistake – this process is important. It's more than important – it's vital. *It creates the possibility for complete healing to come into your life.*

Then, when you begin to feel the first stirrings that true healing might actually be possible, move on to the steps and see the full-force of your power when you align right action with right thinking. You will become an unstoppable force.

When you are feeling lost, afraid, or confused, when you start to question whether or not all of this is really worth it, when you doubt yourself, when you let the beliefs of society overtake your own inner-truth, come back to this spot right here and allow me to hold the vision for your own healing for you, until you feel strong enough to pick it back up for yourself. Read this to yourself over and over again and imagine me, or your best friend, or your mom, or a spiritual being sitting across from you, speaking these words to you. Let them wash over you until you feel yourself begin to calm. Until they start to sound like truth. Feel the support and love and faith that is here for you.

You are not alone. I have walked this path and healed my own illness and so can you. What is possible for one is possible for all. You can feel safe in your own body. You can heal your brain, your body, and your broken heart. You are a powerful creator. You are on the right path. I know that it feels lonely and hard right now but you can do this. I see you as healthy and whole. It's okay to stumble, to fall apart, to want to curl into a ball and disappear. But when you're ready, come back and keep going. You are doing it perfectly. I repeat, You ... Are ... Doing ... It ... PERFECTLY. There is no wrong way to walk your path or heal your disorder. Open up to the support and guidance that is here for you. Love is all around you. It's time to live the life you have imagined.

"And the day came when the risk to remain tight in a bud was more painful than the risk it took to blossom."

– Anais Nin

Chapter 4

Step 1 – Heal Your Body So Your Body Can Heal You

"To keep the body in good health is a duty, otherwise we shall not be able to keep our mind strong and clear."
– Buddha

Remember those "what if" questions I asked you to keep yourself open to? Well, here's a good one … What if your bipolar disorder isn't the reason for your "crazy" but is itself a symptom of a body that is out of balance? Woah … just sit with that for a minute. Seriously, take a pause, take a breath, close your eyes, and ask yourself, "What if my bipolar disorder isn't the root cause of my problems but is a symptom of my own imbalance?"

What if all the stuff (or the "crazy" that I affectionately call it), meaning your mania, your depression, your panic, your suicidal thoughts, that feeling that you're crawling out of your skin, your loss of control, your rage, your exhaustion, your, your, your … fill in the blank. What if all of this that has been diagnosed as bipolar and is supposedly happening because of the disorder, is really happening because your beautiful, divine, perfectly interconnected system is out of balance? Your system could be out of balance for an infinite number of reasons and as someone who's been diagnosed with bipolar, you most likely have several areas in your system that are imbalanced. Most doctors today still struggle to understand this concept – that everything that we do, are, believe and experience is connected. Everything we say, think, eat, and feel is related. Your body and mind are a single, dynamic, connected system. Your thoughts, beliefs, attitudes, traumas, life experiences, and stresses all directly relate to your overall health. And what you think, what you say, what you believe, and what you put your attention on most definitely, directly influence your body.

In the docuseries *Broken Brain*, Dr. Mark Hyman says, "Why does the healthcare industry separate diseases into specialties – the answer: our medical institutions and our financial reimbursement systems are founded on outdated ideas of separate diseases and medical specialties. Abandoning these ideas threatens their economic viability and perhaps even their existence. Our medical training reinforces the illusion of separate body systems by training doctors in separate specialties and sub-specialties."

There are mountains of research available to you should you choose to go looking for it – research that will validate what I've come to believe, and that's this: very few of us who are diagnosed with depression, bipolar disorder, anxiety, even schizophrenia actually *are* any of these things. And that's because these diagnoses are just a set of symptoms that have been lumped together in specific ways so that drug companies can make medications to "treat" the "illness" so that doctors can then prescribe the medications that the drug companies make. Our medical system today is built on the methodology of "Name It. Blame It. Tame It." Institutions are the only ones who benefit from this model – we, the patients, definitely do not. This method of "healthcare" takes all the power away from us and puts it squarely in the hands of companies that are looking to make a profit.

In episode 5 of *Broken Brain*, Dr. Jennifer Love says, "Conventional psychiatry is largely driven by the pharmaceutical industry and managed care. Physicians are under time constraints to only spend a certain amount of time with patients." She goes on to say, "Some of the challenges with conventional psychiatry are that it's really based on symptom management. There's not a lot of research that isn't funded by pharmacologic companies and therefore it's really medication based. Physicians are expected to prescribe medication …"

What I'm asking you to do is to change the question from "What is it?" to "Why is it?" Just sit there for a moment and ask yourself these two questions and feel the wildly different energies behind them. In psychiatric medicine, the first question will only give you a means to manage your disorder – mainly a medication. But it doesn't set up a roadmap to get you better. And it definitely doesn't create the space for healing. But, do you see how empowering the second question is? *Why* are you bipolar? Why are you depressed? Why are you having anxiety or panic attacks? If you know the why of something – it means you then have the power to change it. To truly fix it. To ultimately heal it. This is the space we're going to be operating from for the rest of this book.

Before we go any further I need to put in a disclaimer: I am not a doctor and I am obviously not your doctor. The steps I'm about to walk you through are not a prescription. I am not – in any way – recommending that you suddenly stop your meds. If your intent is to get off your bipolar medications then I strongly urge you to find a naturopathic or functional medicine doctor who will work with you on a withdrawal plan, because stopping your medications will create withdrawal symptoms and it needs to be a process that is monitored closely. What I am also saying and will continue to reiterate throughout this book is that you need to take charge of your own healthcare. You need to become your own advocate. You need to take back your own power and harness your own divine guidance and intuition in order to follow a healing path that is right for you. And it's time. Otherwise you wouldn't be reading this book. So, let's get started!

Now that you know where I'm coming from regarding conventional psychiatry and mental illness diagnoses, let's move onto Step 1, which is rooted in the belief that food is medicine – not just fuel – and takes the approach that when we create the conditions for a healthy brain and body we create a balanced system so that we can then move into the space of true healing.

Change Your Diet

The first part of Step 1 is to change your diet. Science is clear that the biggest and easiest factor under your control to influence your mental health is your diet. There was a trial that was just released in January 2017 that was the first of its kind to show how diet can treat depression. It found that a Mediterranean diet (one that is high in fat, moderate in protein, and low in carbohydrates) put 31% of patients into full remission. There were people in this trial that were already on meds and in therapy, suffering from severe depression – and 31% of them went into full remission by just changing their diet! Unfortunately, most of us don't eat this way. Our westernized diet has evolved to be highly inflammatory – and emerging research is showing that mental illnesses, including bipolar disorders, are deeply rooted in the body's inflammation response.

We're going to take a two-pronged approach to implementing a diet that will reduce inflammation and support your healing. The first prong is to remove the biggest offenders for an unhealthy brain, mainly highly processed foods. The foods to remove from your diet are:

- Gluten (especially highly processed starches, flours, and carbohydrates). Gluten is the glue-like protein found in wheat. Most flour is bad for the body because of the ways it's processed. Our wheat today looks almost nothing like it did 100 years ago and it has been so heavily manipulated and modified that our bodies do not recognize it as food. When digested or partially digested, gluten makes its way through the lining of the gut and into the blood stream; it triggers the inflammatory response in the brain and immune system – which can then trigger a panic attack or a bipolar episode. Eliminating gluten is easier than you think and there are lots of options available now that support a gluten-free diet. Beware of processed foods that are labeled "gluten-free" as they may be made with other chemically derived, sugar-laden ingredients. Naturally occurring grains and starches that are gluten-free are: amaranth, arrowroot, buckwheat, millet, potatoes, quinoa, rice, sorghum, and teff.

- Dairy (mostly cow dairy and especially non-organic dairy). Unfortunately, most dairy on the market today is a highly-processed food. Dairy can be a challenge for many suffering with chronic conditions due to the way it's processed and the protein casein. Milk, even organic milk, has been found to aggravate depression and other mood disorders. Removing it completely, or at least for the first thirty days of a cleanse, will help to keep your body balanced. If you want to continue to consume milk you may want to consider raw dairy (this is unpasteurized and non-homogenized). Milk alternatives like almond, flax, and coconut are options too. Just make sure to choose one that is unsweetened and organic.
- Refined sugar (including all sugar substitutes). Sugar is in almost every packaged food and has many names, like evaporated cane juice, corn syrup, high-fructose corn syrup, sucrose, maltose, dextrose, and maltodextrin. Processed sugars are seven times more likely to cause

oxidative stress and inflammation than naturally-occurring sugars. Processed sugars also disrupt hormones that are key to regulating your metabolism and your emotional and cognitive functioning and ultimately contribute heavily to your emotional rollercoaster.

- GMOs (Genetically Modified Organisms). I'm not talking about hybridization here – like when genes are spliced together from two different apples to create a new species of apple. What I'm asking you to avoid are foods that have been grown with the use of pesticides, herbicides, and other chemicals that wreak havoc on your entire system. GMOs are designed to kill pests that feed on crops – is it any wonder that they do not support healing and vitality in us? Non-GMO Certification is rising in popularity, so start looking for this when you're shopping. Better yet, purchase organic only or whenever possible. By definition, organic foods cannot be produced with GMOs.
- Food dyes. These have been linked over and over again to the onset and worsening of mood disorders, including depression, ADHD, and bipolar. The best way to avoid these is to buy organic and avoid most packaged foods. Make sure to read ingredient labels on all packaged food products.
- Industrial/factory farmed meats and eggs. Like non-organic dairy, industrial or factory farmed meats and eggs come from animals treated with hormones and fed a diet high in GMO corn. This means that when we consume conventional meats and eggs, we are also

consuming the hormones and GMOs that that animal was exposed to. Look for organic, grass-fed, pasture-raised meats and eggs. Not only will you be helping yourself to heal, but you will be supporting farmers who are raising their animals humanely.

- Processed Omega 6 fats/oils. Like sugar, you will find highly processed oils, like vegetable sunflower, corn, canola, and soy, in almost all packaged foods. These oils are considered processed because of the high-heat and chemicals that are used to extract them and because many are made with GMOs. Our bodies do not recognize these oils and they also trigger an inflammation response in the body. Use oils like avocado, coconut, and olive instead.
- Alcohol. I'm not saying you will need to be sober for the rest of your life, but during this healing phase your body will be best supported by not consuming anything that chemically alters your moods. If you have relied on or abused alcohol to help manage your disorder, you will find that it is no longer necessary as you continue to heal and balance.

These foods wreak havoc on your body, brain, and gut. They can trigger anxiety, depression, brain fog, fatigue, irritability, memory loss, and a whole host of other brain functions. I recommend that you eliminate all of these for at least thirty days.

The second prong we're going to focus on is what to add into your diet. These are the foods that will reduce inflammation and support full system healing:

- Healthy fats (like avocados, nuts, coconut oil, wild-caught fish, grass-fed meats, eggs, and butter)
- Bone broth (homemade, store bought, or even in a protein powder form)
- Fermented foods (kombucha, sauerkraut, kimchi, kefir)
- Dark, leafy greens (spinach, kale, broccoli, etc.)

I cannot stress the importance of healthy fats enough. We have been served a load of crap from food companies as well as our own government organizations that supposedly exist for the sole purpose of keeping us healthy. The low fat/no fat movement of the 90s was one of the greatest lies we've ever been told. Our bodies, our brains especially, need healthy fats to exist. Fat is nourishment to the brain and for brain development. 99% of Americans have an omega-3 fat deficiency and doctors believe that omega-3 fatty acids have the potential to treat bipolar disorder because they can alter brain signal pathways in ways similar to mood stabilizers. Postmortem examinations of bipolar patients have found significantly lower DHA concentrations in the prefrontal cortex compared with the general population. Remember though to avoid refined fats and vegetable oils, which have been shown to be linked to depression, violence, homicide, suicide, and even poverty.

I know how intimidating and confusing it can be to change your diet. I'll never forget the first time I walked into a Whole

Foods Market – it seriously scared me. I was in the beginning stages of healing my bipolar and found myself drawn to doing a cleanse. It was one that I had seen on Oprah called The Quantum Wellness Cleanse – where you cut out all sugar, gluten, alcohol, caffeine, dairy, and animal proteins for an entire month. I had never eaten like this – I was raised as a fast food kid. And during that cleanse I bought and made food I had never heard of before. My point is – please don't think that I'm asking you to do something that I haven't or that was easy for me. My first cleanse started me on a path of seeing the direct correlation between what I put in my body and how I feel, how I act, my energy level, and my overall brain function. And make no mistake – I saw massive changes during those thirty days.

This is your first step on your path to becoming bipolar-free: find a diet plan that resonates for you and stick with it for thirty days. Try The Quantum Wellness Cleanse, consider the paleo or Mediterranean diet or give Whole 30 a try. My recommendation would be to do Whole 30; it's the most comprehensive and it's the one I use when working with my clients. In fact, I use a custom-designed meal plan for my clients that incorporates principles from a keto diet and The Whole 30. If you're looking for a book to walk you through this diet, I recommend, *THE WHOLE 30: The 30-Day Guide to Total Health and Food Freedom* by Melissa Hartwig and Dallas Hartwig. Whichever cleanse you pick, keep in mind the above lists of foods to avoid and foods to incorporate, then stick with that plan for thirty days. Keep a mood, energy level, and sleep tracker going during this time so that you can quantify the changes that will occur – because changes will occur. The first few days can be difficult, so make sure that you are practicing good self-care. By the beginning of the second week you will start to notice some significant changes including less brain fog, reduced anxiety, and an increased, sustainable energy. Then, at the end of your thirty days, decide which foods, if any, you want to add back into your diet. Add one type of food back in at a time so you can gauge your body's reaction. Be aware of any food that causes discomfort in your body, diminishes your energy levels, raises anxiety, or triggers a full-blown episode. I recommend only introducing one new food/category per week so that you can fully experience how each food affects you. This approach is called an elimination diet – Google it, you'll find lots of way to support yourself during this process.

As you add foods back in, you may find that you're okay with dairy – or maybe only goat's milk and cheese but not cow's. You may find that organic, sprouted grains are okay for you, or that gluten truly does set off a chain reaction in your body that triggers an episode. Refined sugar should remain a very limited part of your diet and some people find that it's best to keep sugar out of their diet completely. I promise you that your taste buds will change and that the cravings will subside. Food dyes, processed vegetable oils, factory farmed meats, and GMOs should be avoided at all costs. This is because of the added chemicals that you ingest when eating these foods and the ways in which these chemicals have a documented effect on mood states and mental illness. As a side benefit to balancing your moods, you'll find that you're sleeping better, have more energy, are more clear-headed, and you will probably drop a few pounds.

Heal Your Gut

Part 2 in the Step 1 process is to heal your gut. Sounds funny I know, to talk about the gut in relation to your mental health, but there is so much evidence available to us now that explains the gut-brain connection and how and why the health of your gut, specifically the microbiome of your gut (think healthy bacteria) has a direct correlation on brain health. Kelly Brogan says in *A Mind of Your Own* that, "We owe much of our mental illnesses … to life-style factors and undiagnosed physiological conditions that develop in places far from the brain, such as the gut and the thyroid." She goes onto say that, "While it may seem odd to talk about the gut-based immune system in terms of mental health, the latest science reveals that it may be the body's – and mind's – center of gravity" and finally, "Put simply, your microbiome influences practically everything about your health, including how you feel emotionally, physically, and mentally."

I'm sure you've heard phrases like, "I have a gut feeling about this," "gut instinct," or "trust your gut." Turns out these phrases aren't coincidences – our guts really are our second brains. "Our gut microbiome plays a vital role in our physical and psychological health via its own neural network: the enteric nervous system (ENS), a complex system of about 100 million nerves found in the lining of the gut. The ENS (gut) is created from the same tissues as our central nervous system, CNS (brain) during fetal development." (http://www.mindful.org/meet-your-second-brain-the-gut/) Therefore, these two systems really do have many overlapping chemicals, neurotransmitters, and functions and they truly do operate in partnership.

What factors negatively impact the gut and how can we mitigate them? Antibiotics are probably the most commonly thought of culprit when it comes to factors that kill off our good bacteria. But things like highly processed foods, environmental toxins, a lack of nutrients, and relentless stress also can destroy our delicate gut microbiome. It's imperative that you heal your gut if you truly want to heal your bipolar disorder. Healing your gut is also not just about adding in good bacteria through the use of probiotics and fermented foods – it's also about healing the gut itself. Leaky gut is a common condition where undigested protein, like gluten, toxins, and microbes can pass into the bloodstream through gateways that have been created in the intestinal wall. When these particles enter the bloodstream, they cause system-wide inflammation and can initiate an immune response in the body. Over time, leaky gut can lead to mental health issues, including bipolar. Here are the supplements I recommend you use to heal your gut. I have these listed in order of importance – and, in my program the first supplement I have everyone start taking is a high-quality probiotic.

- Probiotics: choose a probiotic that has a high CFU count, at least 50 billion. Also look for one that contains multiple strains of bacteria.
- Enzymes: look for a full spectrum enzyme supplement that contains protease, amylase, lipase, and lactase. Take it directly before or after your meal – especially if you're eating meat, gluten, or dairy.
- L-Glutamine: this is an essential amino acid and is anti-inflammatory. It is helpful in repairing leaky gut.

- Betaine HCL: this boosts your stomach's ability to digest food, especially if your stomach doesn't produce enough acid on its own.
- Collagen powder: only necessary if you're not drinking bone broth on a regular basis. Collagen helps boost your gastric juices and aids in restoring the integrity of your mucosal lining.

One final word on gut health: if you're on an acid-reflux medication, either prescription or over the counter, you are shutting down your body's ability to create acid and digest your food. Hopefully you will see that by changing your diet and healing your gut you no longer need these medications. Stomach acid is a normal and important part of our biology. It is critical for a healthy digestive system. The last thing you want to be doing as you go through this healing process is shut down a biological function that is responsible for ensuring you digest your food and assimilate vitamins and minerals properly.

Add in Supplements

After getting your diet in order and repairing your gut, you can begin adding in supplements that will support the rebalancing of your brain and body. Below is a list that I suggest. Note that I am not recommending that you take all of these and definitely don't start taking all of these at once. The exceptions to this are the first five – they can be taken at the same time and you should begin them around the same time you start your food cleanse. Everything else listed is optional and may come and go as part of your supplement regimen. This is where it's going to be imperative for you to become your own healthcare advocate – check in with your intuition – see which supplements truly resonate for you. Muscle testing can also be helpful – muscle testing is a great tool to use that allows your body to actually tell you what it needs. We'll explore more later about how to tune into and understand the ways our bodies communicate with us.

- Multivitamin: most multivitamins that you find at a big box or drug store are not going to cut it. These are mainly synthetic and your body will not digest or assimilate them in any way. Look for food-based multis that are typically created through a fermentation process.
- Omega 3: look for one that has at least 1,000 mg of EPA & DHA per serving. EPA and DHA are the essential fatty acids found in cold water fish; our bodies do not produce them on their own, we need to eat foods that contain them and supplement appropriately. My personal recommendation is to get at least 4,000 mg per day, either through food or supplementation. Ensure that your supplement is sustainably sourced and is certified from a third-party for freshness. You also want one that breaks down the ratio of EPAs to DHAs; it should be a three to two ratio of EPA to DHA.
- Vitamin D3: I recommend taking between 5,000 – 10,000 IUs daily.
- Coenzyme B Complex: my favorite is from Country Life. Don't take them too late in the day as they can be energizing. Vitamins B12 and B6 are two of the most

important vitamins for mental health – if you choose to not take a B complex then make sure to at least supplement with B12 and B6.

- Magnesium: the one I've taken for years is Magnesium Glycinate 400 from Kal. This is a good one to take in the evenings as it does have an overall calming effect.
- CBD: the full name is Cannabidiol and it is a phytocannabinoid found in plants; the most popularized being from Hemp, which is the non-psychoactive (meaning it doesn't get you high) member of the Cannabis family. We have CBD receptor sites located throughout our bodies (CB1 Receptors are primarily found in the Brain and Central Nervous System; CB2 Receptors are primarily found in the Immune System and Gastrointestinal Tract). By taking a CBD supplement we can balance or 'turn on' our CB receptor sites and essentially bring our bodies back to balance or homeostasis. CBDs have been shown to have antipsychotic properties and early research is showing that CBD can support people with bipolar disorder, anxiety and depression. I started taking a CBD supplement recently and have noticed significant improvements in my overall ability to regulate my mental capacities.
- Turmeric: in the Curcumin form. This orange colored plant is in the same family as ginger and decreases inflammation naturally.

- Trace Minerals: I use ConcenTrace from Trace Minerals Research. It's a liquid that you can put in your water and drink throughout the day.
- 5-HTP: this is most helpful in tapering off medications.
- Apoptogenic herbs: like Holy Basil, Ashwagandha, Rhodiola, Milk Thistle, Rosemary, Astragalus, and Schisandra. Herb companies like Herb Pharm make brain and mood blends using a variety of these types of herbs.
- Amino acid complex: another one to take if you're planning on tapering off medications.
- Evening Primrose Oil: made from the seeds of the flowers of the Evening Primrose plant. It's high in omega-6 oils.

Purchasing supplements from True Hope is also an option. In my experience, they are an amazing company to work with and will support you on your path to becoming medication-free, if that's your ultimate goal. They've expanded their offerings since I've utilized them, but they still have their flagship supplement, Empower Plus, made specifically to treat bipolar disorder.

Reduce Exposure to Toxins

The final part in our Step 1 process is to reduce your exposure to harmful toxins in your environment, including in your home and personal care products. You may be asking yourself what your shower cleaner, perfume, or laundry detergent have to do with your mental health. The answer is – way more than you ever thought, and science is now validating how destructive these chemicals truly are. This is an area that we will never be perfect in – harmful toxins are unfortunately everywhere. They are in our water supply, the air we breathe, and the food we eat – especially if you're eating processed or conventionally-grown foods that are genetically modified. So, we're never going to be able to completely eliminate our exposure to these harmful chemicals. There are areas we can control though, mainly with the products we buy to clean our houses and wash our clothes and with the lotions and potions we buy to keep ourselves clean, looking radiant, and smelling good. The chemicals found in most home and personal care products disrupt our endocrine system, which is the chemical messenger system of our bodies consisting of our hormones. The main endocrine glands are the thyroid and the adrenals. These hormone systems communicate directly with our brains and carry signals to the rest of our body. The chemicals found in common household and personal care products are endocrine-disrupting and bind themselves to our hormone receptor sites, causing similar reactions that a hormone would. What this boils down to is that these chemicals are messing with your body in truly destructive ways and have the very real possibility of starting a chain reaction in your body that could result in a bipolar episode. Here is a list of chemicals to avoid:

- BPAs
- Phthalates
- Pesticides
- Sulfates

- Synthetic fragrances – often labeled Parfum or Fragrance in personal care ingredient panels
- Triclosan
- Parabens
- SLS
- Aluminum

The best way to avoid these chemicals is to shop for products in a natural foods store as they typically will not carry items that contain them. A great resource is the Environmental Working Group; their mission is to "empower people to live healthier lives in a healthier environment." For a full list of harmful chemicals, visit the Environmental Working Group's website, www.ewg.org. Or better yet, download the EWG Healthy Living app, which allows you to scan the UPC barcode of any product and see EWG's safety score. It will tell you why that product got the score that it did and which ingredients in that product are harmful and why.

The added benefit of reducing your exposure to toxins is that it will dramatically affect your gut microbiome. In addition to throwing your hormones out of whack, harmful chemicals kill off your good bacteria. Remember that our systems are completely interconnected, so improving one area of your body will have a beneficial result on others.

Do the best you can here. You don't have to replace every single product in your home. Each time you run out of a cleaner, face cream, or dryer sheet – do your homework and look for a natural option. There's lots of great ones to choose from! Stay with me – don't let yourself get overwhelmed with getting this perfect. Remember, one step at a time. This chapter is the most data-heavy of the entire book. Others will be more experiential. Start with an elimination diet using The Whole 30 plan – this step alone is going to have a profound impact on your overall health. Then work to rebalance your gut, add in the right supplements, and reduce your exposure to environmental toxins. These steps will create the solid foundation you need to fully heal your disorder. Go back to the last chapter and remind yourself that this is worth it, that nothing is more important than healing your disorder, that you've got this – and you're not doing it wrong – and that true healing is truly possible.

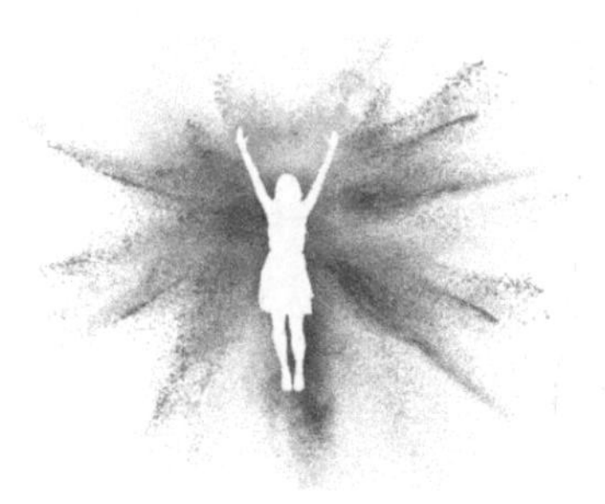

Chapter 5

Step 2–Reset the System– Finding Your Balance and Rhythm

"In the beginning it is always dark. The mind thinks (and leads us to believe) that this darkness is forever. But the body can feel the light, and as soon as it's allowed will always grow toward it."
– Amy Jirsa

Step 1 was all about healing the chemistry of the body. Step 2 is about bringing balance and a natural rhythm back to it. A bipolar mind and a bipolar body are nothing if not out of balance – so we're setting the foundation for true healing by rebalancing. For a lot of us, myself included, this was not a process of rebalancing but of balancing for the first time. I spent my life out of balance and it started with the traumas that I experienced in childhood, which continued into adolescence and young adulthood. I didn't have anyone to mirror for me what a balanced body truly looked like – there was no one in my family who was in balance to teach me and show me the way. I had to learn it for myself.

Everyone's state of balance can be radically different. What feels balanced in my body can feel like discomfort in another's, or chaos, or dread, or anxiety. So throughout this chapter I will offer options you can explore to find balance in your own body. It will be up to you to experiment with the methods I offer to see which ones feel right for you. In my program I really encourage my clients to play with these options and to develop a curiosity about what feels right to them. This concept of being connected to your body so that you can truly feel and hear the messages it's sending you and the guidance it's offering will be further explored in future chapters. The steps in this chapter will help put you back into a natural rhythm so you can begin a right relationship with your body in order to understand the messages that it's sending you – every moment of every day. Your body is always talking to you and it is your biggest champion and greatest navigational tool to creating an amazing life.

We're going to focus on the Big 3: sleep, meditation, and exercise. Creating healthy habits around these three things will have the ability to heal you in ways that the pharmaceutical industry only dreams of. I will offer other techniques and balancing methods – but nothing compares to these three and ultimately – all other options will support the Big 3 in some way.

Sleep

Let's start with the most important and oftentimes the most elusive: sleep. The amount of research available on the importance of quality sleep is immense. For those of us suffering from a mental illness, sleep becomes something that we must conquer. It is a constant fight to get quality sleep. Even when we're exhausted and lying in bed for days, sleep can elude us like a cruel joke. Sleeping for less than seven or eight hours per night though, has dramatic, documented, negative effects, ranging from everything from diabetes to weight gain to memory loss to mental illness. I don't think I've ever met a bipolar person who wasn't also on sleep medications. People suffering from insomnia can literally experience psychotic episodes and lose all control over their thoughts and emotions. The foundation of a balanced body – a body that's in the right rhythm – is solid sleep.

In order to create a solid sleep cycle that will truly nourish and balance the body, I recommend these steps:

- Create a sleep routine: Go to bed and get up at the same time every night and every day, including the weekends. There will come a time when you can be less diligent about this – but to begin, it's important to go to bed at the same time every night and wake up at the same time every morning. Ideally, you should try to be in bed between 10 p.m. and 11 p.m. every night. You will be training your body and your mind to sync up and get with this new program. In order to prepare your body to get on board with going to sleep at the same time every night, I suggest the following:

- Get off your phone! And your computer. And even your tablet. The blue light that these devices emit affects our natural sleep/wake rhythm. Additionally, being on your phone or checking email, or reading the news on your tablet, keeps your brain in the "ON" position and causes a chain reaction for the stress response to stay active in your body. So, I repeat, get off your phone. Don't use any electronics at least an hour before bed.
- Create bedtime habits. This isn't just about getting your body into a relaxed state – it's about literally reprogramming your brain and your body. Things to try include, setting aside at least thirty minutes prior to your designated sleep time as your 'get ready for sleep time.' Use this time to unplug. Take a bath with Epsom salts, do breathing exercises, read a book, drink a cup of tea, meditate, pet your dog or cat, turn the lights down, light a candle … you get the gist. Create a routine that feels calming and restorative to your body – and then follow it *every* night. Even if you're not tired, even if you're exhausted and can't move, even if all you want to do is zone out in front of the TV – especially if all you want to do is zone out in front of the TV. Follow your new bedtime routine. Retrain your brain and body to this new routine and soon enough they'll start preparing for sleep the moment you start it.

- Cut out all ambient light from your bedroom. Put your phone on airplane mode. Use a sleep mask or room darkening shades.
- Keep your room a sacred space – sleep and sex only. If you have a TV in your room, get it out NOW. Don't work from bed – ever. This is further going to train your mind and body that when you're laying down in bed, it's sleepy time. Or sexy time – but it's definitely not 'answer email time', 'scroll through Facebook time' or 'watch *The Late Show* time.'
- Get an essential oil diffuser and run it during your bedtime routine and throughout the night (most have a timer or automatic shut off function). Remember to only use real essential oils – nothing synthetic. My favorite brand is Pranarom. Lavender is probably the most well-known essential oil – but there's a few that help with calming, like Vetiver, Chamomile, Ylang Ylang, Bergamot, Sandalwood and Cedarwood. Most essential oil companies will also make a sleep blend, like Sleep Aid from Pranarom.

- Sleep supplements: even with a solid bedtime routine it can still be impossible – especially in the beginning – to fall asleep and stay asleep. There's a few things that I recommend:
  - Melatonin: this is one that you should not use every night and hopefully you won't need it for long. Melatonin is a naturally-occurring hormone in your body that is produced at nighttime, as the sun goes down, and it's there to help your body relax and

move into sleep mode. However, if your hormones are shot – which with bipolar disorder is most likely the case – then taking a melatonin supplement can be helpful. This is something that will help you fall asleep but not necessarily stay asleep. So, if you have a habit of waking up throughout the night, you may want to try something else or in addition to melatonin. Natural Factors has a product called Tranquil Sleep and it combines melatonin with 5-HTP and Suntheanine (which is their trademarked name for L-theanine). These three together work on the total hormonal system and will help you fall asleep and stay asleep for the entire night. One thing to note here is that if you're waking up between 2–3 a.m. every night this is most likely not a sleep issue – it's an adrenal issue. The steps in this book will help you get your adrenals back on track so over time you should see significant improvements with this. Most clients that I work with also have some sort of adrenal or thyroid imbalance as well. You can also go back to chapter 3 and look at the adaptogenic herbs I recommend – these are great for rebalancing the adrenals.

- Homeopathics: Homeopathy is a medical system rooted in the foundational belief that 'like cures like'. By definition, it is "the treatment of disease by minute doses of natural substances that, in a healthy person would produce symptoms of disease." Homeopathy dates back to the 1700s and is still, to this day, one of the most widely-used medical systems on the planet. Homeopathics are great because they do not have counterindications with other drugs. Quietude by Boiron or Calms Forte by Hylands are two good ones to try. You can also work with a homeopathic practitioner in your area. Flower essences also fit into the homeopathic family and Bach makes a popular sleep aid called Rescue Remedy Sleep.

- Herbs: Valerian, Ashwagandha, Magnolia, Passionflower and California Poppy are good ones. My all-time favorite natural sleep aid (and I've tried a lot of them) is Bed Time by Herb Pharm. It helps me sleep through the night and I never wake up feeling drugged or hung over.

There are a few other things that I want to make note of regarding sleep. The first is that if you're doing all these steps but still getting into bed and not falling asleep – then get out of bed and go do something that relaxes and calms you. Do not get on your phone or do anything else that energizes you. Listen to some calming music, go meditate, do breathing exercises, do mild stretching – only things that keep you in a relaxed state. You don't want to get your brain and body moving back into "Go" mode. Try something for twenty or thirty minutes, then go lay back in bed. Keep doing this until you fall asleep. The second note is that everything else that I suggest in this book will also support a solid sleep cycle. Remember that your body is one big interconnected system – so, things like good diet, exercise, grounding practices, a feeling of accomplishment with your day, and light therapy will all assist you in getting a good night's sleep. So be patient with yourself. Try not to get too frustrated when you find yourself tossing and turning. Tell yourself that it's safe, that you're getting the sleep that you need, and that you are allowed to fully shut down now and go into rest mode.

Meditation

Meditation is the second most important thing you can do for yourself; as such, you're going to see me talk about it throughout the book. The effects of meditation will positively impact every single area of your life and have a tremendous effect on rebalancing the body, retraining the mind, and connecting you to your true self, and will ultimately allow you see yourself as separate from your bipolar disorder. This quote from Lao Tzu captures beautifully what I believe to be meditation's most impactful benefit, putting us back in touch with ourselves, "At the center of your being you have the answer; you know who you are and you know what you want." Meditation takes us to the center of our being. I could write an entire book just on meditation but for this book I'm going to walk you through the basics and explain why a meditation practice is so important to a mentally ill brain.

Psychiatry is finally lending credence to the important role that meditation can play in managing mental illness. Meditation affects our systems on a physical, emotional, mental, and spiritual level.

Physically, meditation literally cools down the inflammation response in the body. And, as I said earlier, inflammation is showing to be the root cause of all chronic disorders, including bipolar and other mental illnesses. Epigenetics is now proving that meditation has the capability to literally rewire our genes and heal the chemistry of our bodies. Additionally, meditation will take your body out of the almost constant fight or flight mode that we've come to live in and put you back into a state where your body can transfer its energy from keeping itself safe to using energy as fuel for healing and rejuvenation. The stress response, or the fight or flight mode, keeps your body focused on its own safety and doesn't leave any energy for true healing and rebuilding. Over time, we can become addicted to that state of stress – more specifically, to the hormones that that state of stress creates.

Emotionally, meditation allows us to not only get a break from the constant yo-yo of our own emotions but to begin to separate from them so that we can see that we are not our emotions. It allows us to become The Witness of our emotions instead of identifying as our emotions. Our emotions are a side effect of our outside world and we are not a slave to them. Through meditation, I've been able to get to a place where I notice emotions as they come up for me and then bring a curiosity to them instead of a judgement or fear, "Oh, I'm feeling anger again. I wonder why this is coming up? What is this anger trying to tell me?" "What do I need to pay attention to or change?" We'll delve into this concept more fully in Chapter 6. For now, just know that you are not your emotions, you don't need to fear them, and they no longer have to run the show.

For people with bipolar disorder I know that this is a radical thought because your emotions have been in charge for so long. Meditation will help you start to see yourself as separate from them so that you can show up less reactive in your life.

Mentally, meditation helps you to become the master of your thoughts. You begin to see that your thoughts are not your truth. They are subconscious beliefs and tools that the mind uses to keep you in a place that is familiar and safe and to reinforce what you subconsciously believe to be true. Meditation will help to show you the habitual thought patterns that float through your mind in any given moment. It will also create the space that allows you to actively choose thoughts that serve your highest good instead of letting your thoughts run the show and keep you from the life you truly want.

Finally, on a spiritual level, meditation has the power to put you back in touch with your own higher self so that you can align to the full power of your own Being and become the ultimate creator of your own life. Meditation puts you in a space where you can finally hear the voice of your own spirit. This is the truth of who you are and when you are able to connect with it you'll see for yourself just how life changing it can be. And your higher self is going to tell you that it has absolutely no desire to remain in a state of illness.

If you're new to meditation, please be gentle with yourself as you move into this practice. And know that it is *always* a practice. I've been meditating on and off for years and still have days where it's almost impossible for me to sit there – my mind is jumping around all over the place, which triggers my body, so much so that I feel like I'm almost crawling out of my skin.

Just keep telling yourself that it's okay and that you're safe. Tell your body that, "We're going to stick with this anyway. You can throw a fit. It's okay. I'm going to stay right here and we're going to complete this quiet time that we committed to." Know that your body may continue to throw a fit. It's all okay. Your mind is going to create a million and one things that are of the utmost importance to deal with RIGHT NOW … that's okay too. Just stay with it. The goal here is not to quiet the mind, although with practice you will be able to do that. It is to build awareness around your own emotions and thoughts, connect you to yourself and strengthen your ability to bring yourself back from unconscious thoughts, behaviors and beliefs that are negatively impacting your life. There are days when I get out of meditation and I feel like I just went ten rounds in a boxing match. But that is so rare for me now; these moments happen less and less as you build your practice. And, as you continue to get more skilled in the art of meditation you'll see the magic of this practice unfold for you in deep ways.

There are 1,001 ways to meditate and every one of them is valid and right. Below are options you can experiment with. See what works for you and get rid of whatever preconceived notions you have about meditation. It doesn't have to be sitting cross-legged on a pillow, wearing white, chanting OM. But if that's what creates magic and meaning for you, go for it! You don't even need to call it meditation, you can think of it as a mindfulness practice, your quiet time or centering.

My personal method of meditation is to sit in a chair with my feet on the floor (because this helps ground me) and listen to binaural meditation music (the app I use is AmbiScience from

Tesla). I focus on my breathing (deep in and out breaths through my nose) and silently repeat the affirmation "Here. Now," because I'm asking my whole system to come into alignment in this present moment. I do this for around thirty minutes each day as part of my morning ritual. And most days now, I get to that sweet spot where I'm no longer trying to meditate and move into a blissed-out state of just "Being." But, some days are different, I don't listen to music because I'm really needing to hear my own breath, and other days I need a longer affirmation because my mind needs something meatier to grasp onto. The key is to commit to a practice, build structure around it, but allow fluidity within that structure so that you are still able to tap into your own guidance of what's needed in that moment. It's best to commit to a daily practice at the same time every day (again, you're training your brain and body to get with the new program) but allow flexibility once you're in that space and time. Start with 5 or 10 minutes and work up to 20 or 30 or even an hour a day. The more time you can spend in this space, the more aligned you'll be to the new, healthy life you're creating for yourself. And I promise you that the moment will come when your brain and body will quiet completely and you'll break the bonds of your physicality and will move fully into a connected state of flow. From that space, you will feel no connection to being bipolar whatsoever and will truly feel the truth of your own wellbeing.

Here's a few options for you to create your own meditation practice:

- Meditate at the same time every day. Commit to it for at least thirty days. Start with 5 or 10 minutes (go for 10, you can do it!). Gradually build up to 30 minutes or more.
- Use music – build a meditation playlist or download a meditation app. If you are using an app on your phone, make sure to put it in airplane mode so that you can be in a space where you won't be interrupted. Do this even if you don't think anyone is going to call or text – because when you leave your phone on, a part of your mind is going to remain on high alert.
- Focus on your breathing. Meditation can be as simple as this: sit quietly, lightly shut your eyes and focus on your in breath, then your out breath, then your in breath … feel how amazing it is that your breath oxygenates your entire body.
- Find a guided meditation – there's a million options through apps or YouTube. Find one that works for you.
- Try a moving meditation – go take a walk in the woods or on the beach. As you walk, ask your body to become fully present, focus on your breath, try to keep your eyes softly focused ahead of you (so you can still see where you're going) and start to quiet the mind. Every time the mind starts to jump, just bring it back.
- Ideally, you should not meditate laying down in bed. Remember what I said about your bed being for sleep and sex only! Find a different spot to meditate. It should be an upright position if possible – when you're laying down it's typically a signal to the body that it's time to

sleep, which can happen during meditation. Don't stress it if you fall asleep, sometimes it's just your systems way of processing a lot of energy or change.

Don't overcomplicate this. Ultimately, meditation is just sitting in silence with yourself and it gives you the time and space to connect to the truth of who you are. Remember – this is a process and a practice. Be gentle with yourself. You're building a new muscle and developing a new skill.

Exercise

The third most important thing you can do to balance your system is to exercise. Exercise is hailed as nature's antidepressant for a reason – for a million reasons. Exercise is proven to balance your hormones, reduce stress, increase circulation, release endorphins, increase brain health, decrease inflammation, create more restful sleep, stabilize moods … need I keep going? More than these physical effects of exercise, it has the ability to put us intimately in touch with our own bodies. In fact, I would say a more appropriate name for this section could be, 'Mindful Movements' instead of 'Exercise' because the goal is to move your body in deliberate ways that will support your healing. We are meant to move. And breathe. And sweat. Physical movement literally puts us in a state of balance. Research is showing that exercise lowers your risk of becoming depressed and helps stabilize all your bodily functions – including your moods.

Does it matter what type of exercise you do? Not necessarily – except that you need to get your heart pumping. Ideally your exercise routine should have both aerobic and strength/resistance training incorporated into it. And even more importantly than that is the intention that you bring to your exercise routine, both the larger intention you've made to yourself to heal your disorder and the smaller intention that you bring to every single exercise session. What I mean by this is that when you show up to exercise, show up fully. Don't use it as a way to zone out – don't get on a treadmill and binge on the news or *Real Housewives*, get on a treadmill or on a yoga mat or in a pool and be there fully. Invite all pieces of yourself to be there in that moment. Connect to your body. Feel its power and strength. Let your body tell you how it wants or needs to move, give it the opportunity to tell you what will be most supportive to it. Then, allow your mind to drop into your body – for those thirty minutes or an hour it doesn't need to figure anything out. It doesn't need to process anything. It just needs to BE. Feel your emotions quieting. Feel your thoughts calming. Invite your body to come into total balance. Focus on your breath and your movement and allow yourself to fully get into the FLOW.

Exercise vigorously (whatever that means for you) at least three times per week. Again, look for ways to incorporate resistance training and aerobic activity. My go to exercise is hot vinyasa yoga. I began my yoga practice about eight years ago and it has transformed my life in ways I never thought possible. I know my own resilience now because of yoga. I can feel when my body is out of balance now because of yoga. I harness the power of my own breath now because of yoga. But I know this is not the platform for everyone. So, find what lights you up and allows you to get into a state of flow, it could be Aikido, boxing, swimming, hiking or dancing. Find what connects you to yourself, allows the outside world to drop away, quiets your thoughts and calms your emotions. Then when you find it – commit to doing it at least three days per week.

The key with these Big 3 – sleep, meditation and exercise – is to create a routine and stick to it for at least thirty days. I recommend to my clients that they keep a mood, meditation, exercise, energy, and sleep tracker so that they can quantify the shifts that occur for them as they incorporate these changes and bring their bodies into balance.

Other Balancing Tools

Below is a list of other things you can try that are also proven to bring balance and harmony back to the body. See what fits for you, experiment, and play with these. Notice what you notice in your system when you try them out. Keep being curious about how these things can support you on your journey. And listen to your body, it'll tell you what's supportive and what isn't.

- Do a media cleanse. Just like a food cleanse, it can be helpful to do a full media cleanse and eliminate or reduce your exposure to TV shows, movies, music and books that elicit negative emotions. Cutting out the news and limiting your social media time can also be helpful. You can replace low-energy or negative-emotion media with things that uplift and inspire you. I provide my clients with a custom playlist during my program and it supports them in staying in a positive flow.

- Develop a gratitude practice. You can use a gratitude journal or jar or just check in with yourself a few times throughout the day and bring awareness to what you're grateful for. More on the incredible power of gratitude in Chapter 8.
- Get grounded. You can do this both energetically and physically. Get an earthing mat, walk outside on the grass, get EMF mitigators, these are devices that will reduce or block electromagnetic radiation. And, as part of your meditation practice, you can go through a grounding visualization – picture yourself with roots coming out from the bottoms of your feet and going deep into the earth. See your full connection to the earth and how stable and secure you are. See your own belonging and place in this world. Feel the truth of that.
- Light therapy. Use a Vitamin D sun lamp in the morning and a pair of blue light filtering glasses in the evening. Even if you're not on a phone or a computer – our lightbulbs and TVs emit blue light.
- Try Tai Chi, Qigong or Float Therapy (this is one of my favorite tools!).
- Take mindfulness breaks throughout the day. Set alarms on your phone if that helps to remind you. Take a few minutes to do a breathing exercise or a centering practice. Even just a few mindful, deep breaths can make a huge difference in balancing yourself and bringing you back from a full-blown episode. My go-to breathing technique when I'm really triggered is called Square Breathing. It goes like this: breathe in for 6 seconds

(or whatever count feels right in your body), hold that breath for 6 seconds, breathe out for 6 seconds (through your mouth) then hold that for 6 seconds. Repeat until you feel yourself calming and coming back into your body. This usually takes 5–15 rounds for me.

Use what feels right in your body and leave the rest. There isn't a one-size-fits-all approach. What's right in my body may be completely wrong for your body. But do not in any way underestimate the magnitude that these practices, especially sleep, meditation, and exercise, have on balancing your body. Remember that you're not committing to these things because me or anyone else is telling you to – you're committing to yourself, your own well-being, your own healing, and you're making your vision of a healty life more important than anything else.

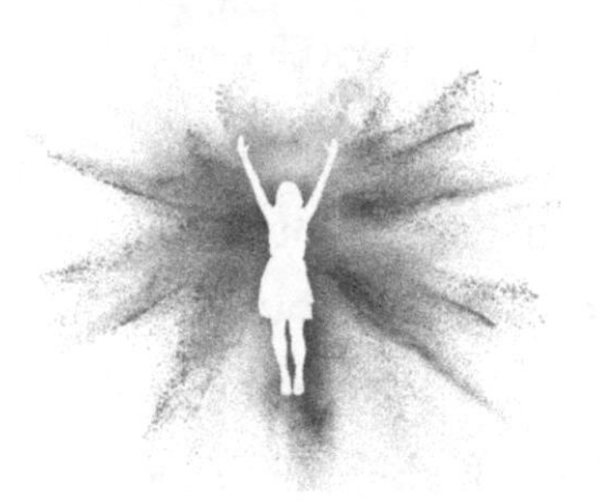

Chapter 6

Step 3 – Let It Go ... Freeing Yourself from Your Own Story

"Don't allow your wounds to transform you into someone you are not."
– Paulo Coelho

I have spent most of my life in one kind of therapy or another. It started when I was very young – my mom put me in therapy when I was about six because I was having night terrors and was unable to sleep in my own room. I know now that the terrors were from the abuse, but I wasn't able to talk about it then and my little mind had no way to process the barrage of mixed emotions that go hand-in-hand with abuse. I didn't mind being in therapy – but it also didn't really help much. And the night terrors continued into my early teenage years. I was unable to sleepover at friends' houses when I was young because I would literally make myself sick. I insisted on staying in my brother's room – even though I had a beautiful room all to myself. My brother still had a bunk bed in his room and I slept on the top bunk, with a desk lamp on the entire night because darkness started a chain reaction of panic.

After years of trying to comfort me through this, my mom finally gave up. I was old enough by this point that I would stay up on the couch and watch TV until the middle of the night because the only way I could fall asleep any longer was if I got to the point where I physically exhausted and couldn't keep my eyes open. No one, not my mom or my doctors or even myself had any idea why I was like this – why I was so terrified. I was about twelve when I could finally sleep in my room, by myself, for the first time. My room was the entire upstairs of a 1 ½ story house. I was on the couch in the living room, watching TV, exhausted – both mentally and physically. I so badly wanted to not be afraid any more – so I worked up my courage to go up to bed myself. The rest of my family had already been sleeping for hours. I slept in my bed by myself that night. I had to do it with a sleeping bag zipped completely around me and the lights on – but I did it. And, still, I didn't know why I needed that comfort of being completely cocooned, zipped in a sleeping bag to my chin, but my body knew that having that layer of perceived protection felt safe.

Of course, I understand my terror now that the abuse has resurfaced and I've learned about the field of somatics, which comes from the Greek word 'soma,' meaning "the living body." Somatic psychology works on the premise that our bodies hold onto past traumas, which are reflected in our body language, posture, and expressions. In certain cases, past traumas can manifest as physical symptoms, such as pain, hormonal imbalance, digestive issues, and even mood disorders, like bipolar. But back then my terror made absolutely no sense to me – or to anyone else around me – and the byproduct of this terror was that my identity of 'the crazy one' was born.

My story is just one example that highlights how our bodies store traumas. Our bodies do the same thing with seemingly small hurts and disappointments too. It doesn't need to be a physical trauma either. The body can store emotional wounds that occur from being told something hurtful about ourselves, losing a parent, not having a need met, or being repeatedly made to feel like we're less-than. The body stores these hurts no matter how big or small and it keeps a record of everything that has ever happened to it – it always remembers, even when we can't. Our bodies become a living record of our entire lives and manifest as our personal body psychology. This means that the body has its own memories and intelligence and will show up in our lives as habitual reactions and patterns.

The reason these traumas stay trapped in our bodies is because at the time that they occur, we don't have the awareness, tools, support, or know-how to heal and release them. So, these pain points lodge themselves into our bodies, only to be expressed in oftentimes imbalanced and inappropriate ways – which can look a lot like a bipolar episode. But, it's not meant to be like this. In the right environment, with the right coaching and support, your body can move through big hurts in the moment so that it doesn't have any emotions left to store. After all, emotions are Energy in Motion and when they have the proper outlet they can arise in us and move up and out freely and easily. When we have the know-how to face the things that bring us pain, we can process them in the moment so that they don't stay lodged in our bodies – and cause us unnecessary pain. But when we hold them in, ignore them, shut them down, or leave the traumas unprocessed, they have no way of moving through, so the body does what it's designed to do and holds onto them for safekeeping until the day comes when we're able to heal, transform, and release them.

At a certain point, I realized that traditional talk therapy was only going to take me so far. Not that it didn't help me at all; in fact, I had two therapists at different points in my life that I still hold in high respect and am very grateful to. Therapy helped me gain a mental awareness of why I was the way I was – but it didn't allow me to move past those learnings in order to be the person I was wanting to become. And I also came to understand that those particular traumas, triggers, emotions, beliefs, and behaviors were coming up because they were truly ready to be released. If I were to hold onto them any longer by continuing to dissect my story, they would never be fully healed. I knew it was time to look forward, find other healing modalities, and transform my past hurts. The beauty of somatic healing techniques is that you don't have to go back in time to sift through your life hurts, you don't have to understand why you are the way you are, you don't have to figure out who caused you pain and why – you just get to listen to and honor your body for what it has endured, then support it in freeing itself and you from a past story that no longer serves you.

This is what working with countless energy healers, somatic therapists, and body workers has taught me. And the process of uncovering, healing, and transforming my own pain points has been, for me, the best way I've found to liberate myself from my past. It has transformed my life in ways that traditional talk therapy could never have come close to. Imagine a world where we taught our kids how to process their painful experiences fully, right then and there, in the moment. Imagine the kinds of adults those kids would grow up to be. Imagine a world where people weren't constantly working their unhealed pain out on each other because their traumas and disappointments were processed and healed when they happened. I firmly believe that if we lived this way there wouldn't be the illnesses we have today, including bipolar disorder.

Sounds incredible to me. And entirely possible. A close friend of mine is an energy healer and a mom of three. The way that she teaches her kids to understand, allow, and process their painful, frustrating, and fearful emotions is one of the most beautiful things I've ever witnessed. She shows them how to be present with their bodies and their emotions so that those experiences and their emotions can fully move through their systems instead of getting stuck, where they'll remain into adulthood and end up coming out in unhealthy ways every time someone or something triggers them.

In addition to our trapped emotions and traumas in the body, we are also dealing with our subconscious minds, which, for the first seven years of our lives, are the only part of our brains that are activated. Our conscious minds do not start developing until after age seven, so everything goes into the subconscious as a record or a program. Think about it this way: for the first seven years of your life you were in the process of downloading information, taking in everything around you, and building the hard drive of your mind. Your thinking brain was not developed, so you had no means by which to process, understand, and contextualize what was going on around you. Everything just became part of your hard-wired program. Your subconscious mind is like a massive control room. It's filled with row after row of cables and hard drives that are the foundation for your entire operating system. And, there's no one actually in that room, there's no one manning the control booth. There's no one to talk to or reason with. It's just a machine. And it operates from a pre-conditioned program and uses proven tactics to keep us 'safe'. These tactics become our habits, and our subconscious programming is constantly working to move us away from things that don't feel good (aversions) and toward things that do feel good (attachments).

This is why it can be so hard to change lifelong patterns and belief systems. We're trying to reason with our brains through ways that it has no means of understanding. This is the reason that talking or yelling at ourselves doesn't work and why it can be almost impossible to change a deep-seated behavior. Therefore, we keep repeating negative behaviors even though they cause us to feel shame, anger and frustration at ourselves. We berate ourselves for not being stronger or smarter. I heard Bruce Lipton use this analogy recently and it made so much sense to me. He went on to explain that we lose our innate power through our programming – that we all start out equally capable of love, equally powerful, equally creative – but the conditions of our lives have created a hard drive that's operating our lives and it doesn't support our inherent beauty, divinity, and power.

So, what do we do about this? And what does any of it have to do with bipolar? The answer lies back in those 'What If' questions. What if your episodes are a result of your body trying to clear past traumas? What if each episode is not actually an episode – but is your subconscious mind and your body trying to heal and release old programs and trapped pain? If that's the case, then how do we free the trapped emotions and traumas of our past and rewire our subconscious programming? Is it even possible? And, what will your life look and feel like if you're able to do it?

Myself and others that I have worked with are here as living proof that it is truly possible to free yourself from your past. Dr. Joe Dispenza says this, "Memory without the emotional charge is called wisdom." This is where I've gotten to – the charge has been taken out of my painful experiences and traumas. This is the reason that I'm able to write this book – because my pain points have been transformed into immense wisdom and experiences that I get to draw from and share.

Below are methods that you can use to free yourself from your own traumas and trapped emotions, transform your habit patterns and ultimately rewire your subconscious mind. I've separated them into modalities that you can do on your own and ones that you will most likely need a practitioner for.

Practitioner-Supported Modalities

Some of these can be done on your own but I found it helpful to start by working with an experienced practitioner so that I had someone there to hold a safe space and to support and guide me as the emotions came up:

- Somatic Psychologist: I worked with one for about a year while the repressed memories of my abuse were coming back to me. This process allowed me to find the spots in my body where I held the trauma of the abuse and it gave my body the opportunity to be a part of the conversation – because our bodies have their own voice and they want to be heard.
- Craniosacral Therapy: this is a form of bodywork that is extremely gentle. It focuses on the wave-like rhythmic pulse that goes through the entire body. I have never felt as nurtured as I did when I was having this work done. For the first couple months my craniosacral therapist couldn't do much more than work at my feet because the rest of my body held so much trauma. My therapist knew within the first session, without me telling her, that I had been abused – because my body was talking to her.
- Myofascial Release Therapy: our fascia is the connective white tissue that links our entire body. Many people find themselves trying this method in the hopes of relieving a physical symptom or to heal from a physical injury. But in my experience, this type of healing was so much more than that. A good therapist will work with you on the physical symptoms but will support the deeper healing that's possible as you allow conscious awareness to be brought to your body and the spaces and places that it's frozen or gripping onto past experiences.
- Breath work: there are many different options here. Find a breath work practitioner near you. The type of breath work that resonates for me is called Soul Breathing and

through this practice I have been able to feel the full 'aliveness' of my own being. Oxygenating the body has the power to free those trapped traumas and to open up energy centers. Once you give breath work a try you'll notice just how often during the day you hold your breath, or breathe shallowly, or use constricted breathing. And as you bring a conscious fullness to your breath you'll see how the breath supports the movement of energy and the release of stored emotions. After a few sessions with a breath work therapist you'll be able to take the techniques you learn and use them on your own, as part of a specific practice or to re-center and ground yourself throughout the day or when you're feeling triggered.

- TRE: Tension & Trauma Release Exercises, otherwise known as 'Shake Therapy.' TRE is "a simple yet innovative series of exercises that assist the body in releasing deep muscular patterns of stress, tension and trauma." My somatic psychologist worked with me on this and I absolutely loved it.
- EFT: or Tapping or Tap Therapy "works like emotional acupressure to quickly, gently and easily release the negative emotions and beliefs that are at the root of all our problems and pain." This is another one that once you have the mechanics down and a full understanding of, you'll be able to use on your own. It's a great method to use, in the moment when you feel yourself get triggered.
- Neuro-Linguistic Programming (NLP): this is a form of therapy whose objective is to bring together conflicting aspects of the self in order to change and heal. NLP

uses the power of storytelling and metaphor to produce results (the visioning and Law of Attraction work we'll do in a later chapter is loosely connected to NLP). The premise of NLP is that when aspects of ourselves are out of alignment or competing with each other, we struggle with dysfunctional, unhealthy behaviors – and that when we change the patterns within ourselves, we can change how we show up in the world.

- Acupuncture: this ancient Eastern healing modality taps into the energy meridians so that they can gently be opened and healed.
- Yoga: as I said earlier, yoga is my go-to physical exercise. But it's so much more than that. It has taught me how to hear my own body and has shown me, in real time, that our bodies truly do store emotions. Anyone who's ever taken yoga has probably heard how our 'hips store a lot of painful emotions' and if you've ever held pigeon pose for longer than a few minutes, you've most likely felt the intense emotions that begin to arise. They can range from rage to pure, blinding grief and everything in between. I've had countless moments in yoga class where I am brought to tears from the emotions that come up when my body is holding specific poses. But the beauty of this practice is that it gives your body the opportunity to release those emotions. This is why when the tears come, I don't hold them back. I let myself lay there in pigeon pose and quietly sob, give thanks for the release, and honor my body for all that it has had to endure. Yoga can obviously be done on your own,

anytime, anywhere. But starting out it may be helpful to find a yoga instructor, class or studio that resonates for you so that you can learn how to correctly put your body into the specific positions. I prefer to do yoga in a class because I love the group dynamics and energy that is created.

- Reiki, Sound Healing, Crystal Therapy, Shamanic Journeying: these are all more energetic or spiritual practices. I've tried them all. There are many different types of energy healers; find one that feels right to you. Stay open to what can happen. I am an empath and channel energy and information myself and use these abilities to assist my clients in their healing work.
- Hypnotherapy: this has emerged as a credible, evidenced-based treatment option for healing all different kinds of traumas. Hypnotherapy unlocks the subconscious mind so that you can see what your triggers are. More controversial is regression hypnotherapy, which allows you to go back to unconscious moments in your history to see where the trauma originated – and through the support of a skilled therapist can heal the trauma at the origination point.

Individual Practices

- Meditation: I talked about this at length in the previous chapter. The benefits of meditation are immense. Meditate every day. Commit to it. Allow it to open up those spaces and places in you that are already healed so that you can use them to create the awareness's necessary to heal the other parts of you that are ready to be transformed and released. As I previously stated, you can't meditate incorrectly but it can take time to get comfortable with meditation and to ultimately 'master' it, therefore, I use several meditation methods and techniques with clients in my program to help them find the right method that works for them.

- Body scanning: sit quietly and go through each area of the body. Start at your toes and work your way all the way up to the top of your head. As you focus on a specific area, tighten then release it so that you can create a physical awareness as well as the mental awareness. Then really tune into it, feel what it's feeling – is it tight, or cold, or do you feel a buzzing, are there any emotions or moods present – then allow it to 'talk to you.' Do free form journaling and see what comes up. We tend to hold most of our traumas in our large energy centers, mainly our sacral and solar plexus areas, along with our hearts or chests, throats, and shoulders. We can also hold a lot of energy in our jaws and brow areas. Let these areas share their stories with you.
- Brain Wave Entrainment (BWE): the premise behind BWE is that you can use certain tools or technologies, like binaural beats, to alter your brain waves for the primary purpose of changing the way you feel. Entrain means "to adjust an internal rhythm so that it synchronizes with an external cycle." BWE can help put your brain waves into frequencies that support sleep, creativity, and calm and the act of entraining brain waves reduces anxiety

and increases the production of "happy chemicals" in your body. This is showing to be a promising tool for the manipulation of cognitive processes and modulating mood states. I use the app AmbiScience by Tesla and I highly recommend it. I typically use the app during meditation or whenever I have overwhelming emotions or am working on or through something big; it helps to regulate my moods and put me into my desired state of being.

- Body movements: we talked about exercise in the previous chapter. True change at its core is a biological process. Our brains alone cannot heal us. Our bodies are meant to flow, express and move and as we allow them to do these they will open up to deeper and deeper states of belonging, stability, healing and joy. Deliberate and mindful body movements will give you the opportunity to build resilience, gain a deeper understanding of who you are and what your purpose is, connect you to your body and give it an outlet to express itself. Body movements are any deliberate practice and are, by their very nature always physical. They can include any 'exercise' practice that allows you to get out of your head, into your body and learn new competencies and include everything from rock climbing, to walking in nature, to dance.
- Let the rage out: one of the greatest things Josh ever did for me was to give me a metal folding chair and a bat and permission to go beat the crap out of it. And, by permission, I mean that he made it okay for me to

truly rage – which is something that is particularly frowned upon in our society, especially for women. At the beginning of my bipolar healing I had immense rage bubbling up and spilling out of me. Beating that chair gave my body an outlet to release it. I used it regularly for a couple months. The chair no longer resembled a chair when I was done with it, but I had freed so many trapped emotions. There are times when I still need to get the rage out and usually do this now by screaming – an all-encompassing scream from the depths of my gut. There aren't many places to do this without scaring your family or neighbors – but I found that doing it while driving on the freeway with my windows rolled up works pretty great. You can also scream into a pillow, but for me, it's more therapeutic if the scream is allowed to fully flow. I also found that underneath my rage was a well of grief. So be prepared: anger and rage tend to be easier emotions for us to face and they usually come out first, only to expose the grief and sadness that lie underneath. These emotions are more vulnerable, so be gentle with yourself, practice lots of self-care, and if possible have someone nearby who can catch you when you no longer have that rage holding you up. Also, prepare yourself for a massive energy shift after you let the rage out. I am typically exhausted afterwards and need to let my body rest, but you may also experience an energy surge. Either way, honor what your body is asking for. Another thing to note here is that you may have completely shut yourself off from your right to own your feelings – so letting the rage out may feel very uncomfortable in your body, at least to begin with. At first, you may only be okay with letting out an emphatic swear word in a loud voice.

- Journal, sing, dance or create in some way. Give your body an outlet to express itself creatively.
- Get curious with the 'bad emotions.' Instead of judging them or shutting them down, develop a practice of asking why they're there. What do they have to tell you, where are they coming from? There is *always* a message or lesson to follow. We'll talk more about this in the next chapter.
- Explore anything else that you feel called to – anything that will help you connect to and bring awareness to your body.

This work that I'm asking you to do in this chapter can be the most painful and difficult out of everything in this book. Martha Beck says in *Finding Your Own North Star*, "If you've never grieved a wound, bringing it into consciousness will make you feel an emotional reaction almost as intense as if the event were actually happening. You may feel sadness or rage that takes your breath away." So, I'm going to say it again, be gentle with yourself. Bring as much love as you can to the work you're doing. Know that you are brave for going through it, for truly facing your hurts and having the courage to transform and heal them. Give yourself lots of space during this work and don't overdo it. Let your body be your guide – it will tell you when it's had too much or if you've gone too far. You are building what's called "Somatic Literacy", which according to Doug Silsbee in *Presence Based Coaching; Cultivating Self-Generative Leaders Through Mind, Body and Heart* is comprised of six fundamental truths. These are: 1) your body shape and movements perfectly reflect your history, stored traumas and programming 2) your body determines your experiences 3) a wealth of sensations is available through your body 4) sensation provides an early warning system for your habits 5) practice through the body allows you to build and stabilize new competencies and 6) joy and fulfillment are body experiences. As you start to reconnect to your body, give it lots of gratitude, love and support for storing these pain points for so long. It's done an amazing job, and it's okay for your body to let them go now. In fact, it's time for your body to let them go so that you can continue moving forward on your healing journey. You're ready and so is your body.

Chapter 7

Step 4 – Your Body Is Always Talking to You ... Will You Listen?

"Your feelings will guide you if you have the courage to tap into them and listen."

– Marie Forleo

As someone with bipolar, the above quote may sound like a load of crap. Because, to those of us who are bipolar, our feelings and emotions oftentimes are scary, out of control, extreme, and all-consuming. And instead of our feelings being something that we allow to act as our guide and lead us toward the light, they are typically something that we try to outrun, avoid, and manage because we've learned not to trust them. What's worse, we've learned to out and out fear them. We've been taught that our feelings, especially the highly-charged ones, are not our own – they are a result of the disorder. So, then we begin to not only fear them and distrust them but to actually resent them. There is still a part of me, sitting here today, having created a completely different relationship to and with my feelings than the one I had when I was suffering from bipolar, that has a negative reaction to the quote at the beginning of this chapter. There's still that part of me that wants to say, "Shut up Marie. Come live in my body for a day and then talk to me about the courage to listen to my own feelings. I'm courageous because I'm still here despite having to do battle with my emotions and feelings on a daily basis."

And there is now a part of me, the greater part of me, that knows that she's right. And that our feelings truly will guide us to the light; in fact, they are always guiding us toward the light. Toward our joy, passion, love, true self, toward a fully-inhabited life and a fully-empowered state of being.

Steps 1–3 were all about beginning to heal what's broken, bringing awareness back to your body, and rebalancing your entire system. Going through those steps is going to shift things for you and create new areas for you to tap into and explore. Martha Beck describes it like this, "The outermost compass [of your North Star navigational equipment], the easiest to access, is your body. If you're out of touch physically, it's hard to reach the next layer: emotion. When you do connect with your emotional compass, you'll immediately bump into any emotional wounds that may be gumming up the works. Heal them and you're left with a set of emotional impulses that will not only tell you where your North Star is but also map out a route and describe the terrain you'll have to cover." This is what we're working toward. This is why we did the foundational work of healing our bodies through diet, supplements, and detoxification, and why we brought balance back to our bodies through sleep, meditation, and exercise. Why we are experimenting with ways to reconnect, or connect to our bodies for the very first time. And, why we are going through the process of uncovering, healing, transforming, and releasing our old wounds. Because, this brave work will connect you to yourself in ways you didn't even know were possible and will create the opportunity for you to begin using the divine resources you've been given – including the ability to understand the language of your body, mainly your emotions and feelings. Moving into this space, you will begin to see that when we use our emotions for the purpose they were intended for, we will always be led toward the light.

This is another area where I'm going to ask you to be open and curious, and to stay in a state of "What If-ness" because it's most likely going to challenge some of your beliefs. It's okay if you feel resistance rising. Acknowledge it, bring awareness to it and ask it why it's there. Be curious about which of your fundamental beliefs is being threatened by this. Here's a key point: you will only feel resistance in your own body when you're truly going in a direction that is not in your highest good or when you're feeling threatened. The threat can be real or perceived – and in most cases, it's perceived, meaning there is no legitimate, immediate threat to your well-being in this moment or in most moments. It's just your mind sending a signal to your body, trying to keep it safe, by tricking it into thinking that by taking this new step you will get hurt in some way. So, again, bring curiosity to any resistance that arises in you.

Here's a "What If" question: "What if there are no good or bad emotions – what if every emotion is simply a response to what's going on and is information you can use to show you how to proceed?" We've been taught that feelings of fear, anger, and sadness are bad and we should do everything we can to avoid them or shut them down, while feelings of joy, peace, and excitement are good feelings and we should be doing everything we can to create more of them in our lives. This creation of good feeling states is something that I support fully and in the next couple chapters we'll look at how to become the intentional creator of experiences that will multiply these types of feelings. But, for now, I want to focus on our judgement of the negative feeling states, because this is where we get ourselves stuck.

When something that we don't want or that doesn't feel good shows up in our lives, we tend to give it *a lot* of attention. We tell everyone about it, we complain about it, we feel sorry for ourselves, we take it on as our own. So, then, the initial negative feeling that first came up gets amplified and we create more negative feelings about it. Pretty soon, we're having negative feelings on top of negative feelings and after a time, we're not even sure why we're feeling bad anymore. That original thing that caused the first bad feeling has long passed – but we're still living in a state of fear or anger or blame or sadness. That initial bad feeling has now become a bad mood and if left unchecked ultimately will become your way of being. Or, it could be that, we're still tightly hanging onto the story of whatever caused that negative emotion so fully that we can recall it like it happened in this very moment instead of two months ago. To compound matters, we are not able to act in our best interests or in our full power when we're feeling like this, so we then add fuel to the fire by doing things that hurt us or others. We're triggered and we lash out or shut down. We revert to old safety mechanisms like alienating ourselves from our loved ones or binge eating or drinking too much. Our old programming and habit nature take over, effectively eliminating our ability to create self-awareness and choose a better feeling path. By this point our body is aligning itself to this "bad" feeling so it may start creating physical symptoms to go along with the emotions; it may develop headaches, or nausea or the flu. In the case of bipolar, it may manifest as a full-blown episode. You see where I'm going with this? Do you see how one negative emotion can turn into a bad week, or month or year, until finally it just becomes your state of being?

Instead of going down that rabbit hole and creating a negative being state, we could have examined that initial emotion when it first came up. We could have brought curiosity and compassion to it. We could have tested out alternatives with the intent of turning that negative feeling into a positive one. We could have questioned it to see what it was trying to tell us and where it wanted us to go or what it wanted us to do. It could have been as simple as just fully allowing that feeling to be expressed and heard and then releasing it.

There are a few key skills to build in order to fully use our own emotional guidance system. The first is to separate ourselves from our emotions. Our emotions (and our thoughts) are not us. We are separate from them – yet we almost always completely identify with them and as them. Think of how often in a day or week or month you make these kinds of statements: I'm depressed, I'm sad, I'm angry, I'm irritated … I am, I am, I am. These are all I AM statements that you're sending out

or judging them as bad (when they're not bad, they're a gift from yourself) you should welcome them, invite them to sit down and have a conversation with you. See what they have to say, see what wisdom they have to impart. GET CURIOUS. Stop judging. Stop stuffing. Stop avoiding. Building this skill, of being present with your own emotions, listening to them and allowing them to move through, has the power to take you out of the bipolar spiral, stop an episode in its tracks, and to ultimately put you back into a balanced state.

Once you've welcomed the energetic and emotional conversation with these feelings, you can continue to use your body as a guide. Start to explore what path is right, take a different approach with that coworker who's ticking you off, stop laying on the couch every night binging on Netflix, stop feeding yourself that thing that makes you feel terrible, stop procrastinating on that project you've been wanting to finish, stop buying into that old story that you're a victim. As you change your behavior, new feelings will come up that will tell you if you're on the right path. Energy will start to build, you may feel a little lighter or a little freer. These shifts can be very subtle – most of them are not going to knock you upside the head, so you need to be fully connected with your body and have quiet space in your day in order to really hear them. Oprah's got it right, "Difficulties come when you don't pay attention to life's whisper. Life always whispers to you first, but if you ignore the whisper, sooner or later you'll get a scream." This to me is how a sad moment turns into an all-out depressive episode or how a bit of excitement or anxiousness can lead you to out of control mania.

So, a big part of the work we're doing here is to avoid those screams at all costs – this has been our world of bipolar, a constant state of screaming. Let's quiet those, start truly listening to where and how we're being guided. Begin to trust those emotions, give them the space to be expressed and accepted. Take the steps to remain connected to your body so you can hear those whispers.

My own practice of listening to the whisper looks like this: I spend time in meditation every day. I pause throughout my day to bring myself back to the present, into my body. I take a few deep breaths. I invite all parts of me to come back to this space and time, Here, Now. I do a quick body scan to see if there's any tightness or anxiety brewing – and if there is I see what it has to say to me. And, when I'm making big decisions I *always* check in with my body first. I do this by giving it both sides of the decision as a statement, for example: "I commit to doing this project that my coworker asked me to do" and, "I don't commit to this project that my coworker asked me to do." I speak each of these to my body and then get quiet and see how my body responds. A negative response for me doesn't actually feel bad – everything just sort of goes quiet and the energy shuts down. A positive response creates energy, I feel it begin to move, to rise up in me, there's an ever-so-slight stirring in my belly and my chest. See, subtle, right? Just a hint of a whisper. But immensely powerful and it *never* steers me wrong. When you start doing this you'll be able to catch yourself, make a change, pick a different path, and avoid a bipolar episode completely.

Here's an exercise you can use to feel how your own body talks to you and to sense what emotions arise for you when you're faced with two opposing choices. Find two different foods, one thing that you love and one thing that you hate. First, sit with the thing you love, feel it, look at it, smell it, imagine eating it and how good it's going to taste. Before you put it in your mouth, notice what emotions are coming up for you. What's going on in your body? Are you feeling excitement? A quickening of your pulse or breath? A stirring in your belly? Then, eat it and notice what you notice again. As you're eating it and fully enjoying it, bring into your mind that other food that you hate. Know that it's coming next. Notice how your emotions and body change. What's coming up for you now? What emotions are present? Even though you haven't actually taken one bite of this thing that you hate and are still in fact chewing the thing you love, have you lost your joy for the thing you love in your anticipation of the thing you hate? Where are you feeling that negative anticipation in your body? This simple exercise shows us a few key things: 1) how easy it is for us to not be present – but to always be in a state of remembering or anticipating, 2) that our bodies are always talking to us, through different sensations and through emotions, 3) our emotions are always guiding us toward what is best for us. Now, try to bring this level of awareness to your emotions in your everyday life. Don't strive for perfection here and don't use this as another way to judge yourself. This, like everything else we're working on, is a practice. You will never get it right 100% of the time and that's okay. I still get triggered by things and people and I have to work to bring myself back so that I can understand what the message is. Sometimes it takes hours or a couple days for me to recognize that I'm identifying as my emotions and that

I've gotten off track. But the difference now is that I always do eventually recognize it and I have the tools to come back, to listen to the guidance that's there for me, and to make conscious choices instead of letting my thoughts and emotions run the show.

We're going to utilize this principle of our emotions as our guide in the coming chapters, so get comfortable with it. Play with it. Create space to connect with your body. I promise you that you can get yourself to a place where your emotions no longer feel like your enemies – but instead feel like the gifts that they are.

Chapter 8

Step 5 – Find Your Joy and Let It Lead You Back to Yourself

"Choose joy. Joy is a choice. Joy is a witness.
Joy is a therapy. Joy is a habit."
– George Foster

Finding your joy, following your bliss … easier said than done, am I right?! If this were an easy thing to do, don't you think everyone would be doing it? Living in joy all the time – sounds pretty amazing and most likely, totally impossible. From where you're standing today – this probably feels farfetched, idealistic, unattainable, like a million miles away from where you're at.

My goal when I was going through the process of healing my bipolar disorder wasn't to create joy, it was just to find some peace, to get to a place where I didn't want to kill myself on a regular basis, bring balance to my life, and to get my emotions to a manageable state. For me, that was as far as my mind and imagination would allow me to go. But what I found as I got through the initial healing process, connected with my body, and released trapped emotions, was that I wanted more than just to feel 'okay.' Not 'more' in the sense of more things or more because I didn't feel like I had enough or wasn't enough but more in the greater sense of the word. More energy, more opportunities to create, more lightness, more of a connection to myself and the world around me – and yes, the desire for real joy began to bubble up. What I came to realize was that I had almost completely shut down my ability to feel joy, that true joy was almost scary to me, that I had cordoned off the areas where my joy resided and that I had almost no reference point any longer for what pure joy really looked or felt like.

Unfortunately, this is something that is all too common, not just for people suffering from bipolar disorder, but for a large part of the human population. We live in a world where pure joy is reserved for children. Most of us exist in a place of just getting through the day, dealing with the next stress, with the next issue, with the next painful moment. We place our focus on things that we think will bring us joy – but find that they almost never do. We buy things, we try to fit into a box so we're accepted, we work for that next promotion, we exercise for the sake of being thin – with the hope that being thin will bring us joy because then people will like us, or it will bring us that love relationship. And when we buy that thing, get that promotion, or lose that weight we feel a sense of happiness or accomplishment for a time, a brief moment really, and then all the old thoughts, fears, and beliefs begin to creep back in. We realize that that moment of joy was fleeting, so we start to look for the next thing that we think will bring us joy. And so on, and so on, and so on, until we have built a belief system around constantly striving for joy but never being in joy. We get programmed to believe that true joy isn't possible, so we settle for a life that just doesn't feel bad. At a certain point, we don't even realize we're settling any longer because that mediocre life, that life that doesn't feel bad but isn't actually centered around joy, has become our truth, the way we see ourselves and the world around us. It becomes just the way things are.

For those of us living with bipolar disorder, this process is taken to the extreme. Because of everything that we've been through, everything we've had to endure, every pain, every loss of control, every disappointment and every heartbreak, we are left with a pile of pain, shame, and resentment that becomes debilitating. So much so that our innate desire to create and inhabit joy is suffocated completely and all hope feels lost. At a certain point, we come to believe that we are inherently unworthy of joy.

But, what I want you to take in as your own truth is that your joy is still there, waiting for you, and no matter what you've been through and no matter what you've done or who you've hurt – you are absolutely, 100%, without a shadow of a doubt, worthy of a life that is filled with joy … and love, and creativity, and passion, and purpose. And that the process of uncovering your joy, of creating and experiencing joy is itself, a step in the healing journey – it's not the destination point. It's something that will lead you to your true healing. I have transformed and released as many traumas through the process of play and reconnecting to my joy as I have through the hard work of transforming and releasing pain through therapy.

So, what do you do, how do you find your joy? You start digging for the light. Think of Steps 1–3 as not only building a foundation for joy and rebuilding a body that can support joy, but of excavating the light. And in Step 4 you learned that your joy, your inner guide, your higher self, is always calling to you and it uses your emotions and the senses in your body as a way of pointing you toward your joy.

Take the practice of creating and inhabiting joy as an important step in your healing journey – because finding and following your joy is healing, transformative, and an act of service to yourself and everyone around you.

For me, when I read something like this or a teacher tells me something like this, I think, "uh-huh, that's all well and good, and sure, I would love to find my joy. But how do I actually do that?" So, I'm going to tell you ways that I have been able to find my own joy. Just like everything else in this book, there is no prescription, it's not a step-by-step process or one-size-fits-all approach. Your journey is your own and it's intimate and individualized. Be your own advocate, take charge over your own experiences, stop giving your power away to something or someone outside of yourself, and continue to build the skillset of listening to the whisper that's always guiding you toward your own best life.

Here are things I've used to bring joy into my life and to ultimately create a life that is filled with joy. Through these experiences, I have become a Being that knows that following my truth is an act of service and always leads to more joy. And, being in the grounded and centered state of joy takes up so much space in my world now that there is no opportunity for a bipolar episode to take hold.

- Meditate: are you getting the message yet? It's time to get good with meditation because it's the foundation for everything. How are you going to be able to listen to the voice that's leading to your joy if you're never quiet enough to hear it?
- Get curious: start paying attention to what you're curious about. Just like that voice that whispers to us, our joys and passions don't always make themselves very clear. It's not like a flashing neon sign, saying "this is it, I'm your joy." But I guarantee you there are things that you're curious about. These are things that catch your attention, that keep popping up into your awareness or that cause a bit of excitement in your body. You won't know until you follow them if they'll lead you to your joy or not. You will always be better for having followed them though because you will then have information that you can use to clarify your desires and get you closer to your joy. Elizabeth Gilbert talks a lot about following your curiosities; here's one of my favorite quotes, "Just follow your curiosity. Trust your curiosity. If something is interesting to you, trust that it is interesting to you for a reason. That it is another breadcrumb on the amazing trail that will make your life yours and not anyone else's. Curiosity above all." Following my own curiosities has led me to yoga, joining groups – where I've made

lifelong friends, developing new skills, getting certified as a coach, exploring new places, and even writing this book. Each of these things created new curiosities for me to examine and have shaped my life in ways I am immensely grateful for. So, get quiet, tune into yourself, bring awareness to what's curious or interesting to you then find the courage to follow it. If you find that it didn't lead you to your joy – it's okay. Be proud of yourself for taking the step, then harness the energy that taking that step created and be grateful for the deeper understanding it provided you about yourself.

- Reconnect to your own creativity: this can be anything, writing, drawing, painting, woodworking, collage making, dancing, singing, pottery, drumming – whatever it is for you, reconnect to it. Most of us have shut down this side of ourselves. It's time to open it back up – remember back to when you were a kid and what you liked to create. If you can't remember what you liked to create as a kid – it's okay, get curious. Start exploring. You can begin very simply. Get some colored pencils and a coloring book – there's a million of them for adults out there now. Find a class to try. Go walk around the art or toy section at a store and see what grabs your attention – then buy it – and play with it. Go to a wine and painting event. One of my very first creative endeavors was to paint plain terra cotta pots. It was such a simple act of creating and transforming but for me, it was rewarding and joyful. Each time you try something, check in with yourself to see how it feels in your body and whether or not your body wants more of that experience.

- Be of service: remember that I said that finding your joy is in and of itself an act of service? Well, then it makes sense that by performing an act of service, you can find and experience your joy. Volunteermatch.org is a great website to use to find volunteer opportunities near you. Getting out of your head, away from your own troubles, and using your body to serve others is one of the greatest ways I've found to bring in more joy.
- Take yourself on play dates: if you have kids in your life it can feel less awkward (especially at first) to go on play dates with them. Reintroduce your body to the joy of figure skating, rolling down a hill, jumping in a lake, or playing at a park. I'm lucky to have nieces and nephews that I get to play with on a regular basis. And for Christmases and birthdays, I don't buy them stuff – I take them on play dates. We've done everything from trampoline parks, to go karting, to laser tag to tea parties. Give yourself permission to really be a kid in these moments. Let the judgements go. Immerse yourself in that experience of play. Not that you need it, but if it helps, you have my permission. Go play. Wild and free.
- Shake it up: try taking a new route to work, go walk around a neighborhood you don't know, pick a city you've never been to and go take an impromptu weekend without any planned agenda, try a new coffee shop, cook a new recipe, invite an acquaintance out for lunch. See what opens up for you as you get out of your

routines. This can be a tough one for people with bipolar – because in a lot of ways, it is our routines that keep us stable. But, through the guidance offered in this book you'll find that it's safer and safer to change things up. Especially when you've created a solid base with the new, healthier routines discussed throughout this book.

- Create a space in your home that is uniquely yours: whether you have kids, a partner, or live with a roommate, find some space that is yours alone. It can be a closet, or a nook, or an entire room. Fill it with things that bring you joy and help you connect to yourself.
- Practice presence: allow yourself to be fully present in whatever you're doing. Keep inviting yourself to come back to the present moment, Here, Now. One of the quickest ways to move out of your joy is to split your energy by thinking about the past or worrying about the future. Multi-tasking has become the norm for most of us and is even a badge of honor – we tout our ability to multi-task on resumes. In truth though, multi-tasking is not only ineffective – it's destructive. So, come on back, to right here, right now. Allow yourself the gift of staying in the flow and remaining fluid.
- Join a group: there's many different ways to go about finding the right group(s) for yourself and we're going to talk through them more specifically in the next chapter. But a large part of finding and creating joy is to get in a space where you can experience it with others.
- Take a class: it could be a language, writing, cooking, or painting class … it could even be an accounting class if

that's what lights you up. But give your brain something else to focus on other than your day in and day out problems. Give it a job, let it use its power to learn something new instead of focusing on what it thinks it already knows.

- Develop a gratitude practice: part of the reason we experience so much pain and suffering in our lives is because we give the most attention to the things that are causing our pain and suffering. Developing a practice of gratitude can shift your focus from what isn't working in your life to what is and put you in a state of coherence so that the Universe can bring you more of what you want, more of what feels good, more joy. Start noticing how much attention you give to negative talk about your disorder and its episodes versus the times when things are balanced and feeling good. There's infinite ways to go about building a gratitude practice; you can create a gratitude jar and throw notes of gratitude in it every day or start a gratitude journal and write 3 or 5 or 10 things in it every night that you're grateful for. These don't have to be big things; you can find gratitude for a day where your emotions didn't overtake you, for the courage you showed to start a new class, for it being a beautiful day so that you could go take a walk. It can be gratitude for the companionship of your cat or dog, or for a friend calling to check up on you or for that stranger that smiled at you as you passed on the street. You can also specifically focus on people who have supported you through your healing journey. Bring them clearly into your mind and heart, feel their support, love and guidance. Allow that feeling to magnify and push out any other feelings of fear, resentment or pain. My gratitude practice has evolved into a way of being – I give thanks throughout the day, focus on the good as it happens, take small moments to acknowledge the good that's coming or the emotions of joy or love or excitement that I'm feeling. I also give thanks for the "bad" feelings because I know that they're from my higher self and are providing guidance. And that when used in this way, I no longer need to fear them, resent them, or shut them down. My gratitude is to the Universe for providing the opportunity and guidance, and to myself for allowing the good to come into my life. Dr. Joe Dispenza's go to gratitude statement is, "Thank you. Bring me more." And I love it so much I have adopted it as my own. Thank you for this moment of peace, bring me more. Thank you for that good night's sleep, bring me more. Thank you for the unexpected $100, bring me more. Thank you for this feeling of aliveness, bring me more. Thank you for the love and support of my family, bring me more. Thank you for this cup of tea, this new experience, this new job, the creation of health in my body and mind … bring me more. Work your way up from a gratitude practice to inhabiting a constant state of gratitude.

Whatever methods you choose, allow yourself to commit to and experience them fully. Remember that the pursuit of joy is a healing practice. In finding your joy you are healing and honoring all those aspects of you that weren't allowed to feel joy in the past. You're honoring that little girl or little boy that was told to sit there and be quiet, who was told that you're not good enough to be an artist, that you needed to grow up or act like an adult. Give that piece of yourself the opportunity to come back out, explore the world and find the joy. This practice will free you and heal you.

Chapter 9

Step 6 – Our Path Is Our Own but We're Not Meant to Walk It Alone

"Find your tribe. You know, the ones that make you feel the most YOU. The ones that lift you up and help you remember who you really are. The ones that remind you that a blip in the road is just that, a blip. They are the ones that when you walk out of a room, they make you feel like a better person than when you walked in. They are the ones that even if you don't see them face to face as often as you'd like, you see them heart to heart. You know, that kind of tribe?"

– Jennifer Pastiloff

Have you heard this one before? *You become like the 5 people you spend the most time with. Choose Carefully.* This has become such a common saying in the coaching world that it's sort of a cliché. Except it's not a cliché – it's a philosophy that has born itself out to be true time and time again and it is now proven that on an energetic level, our systems bring themselves into resonance with the energies around us. So, the energies of your system, your emotional, physical, mental, and spiritual systems are all reorganizing themselves around the energies you're close to in order to put you in a state of resonance. According to Gregg Braden, "In its simplest form, resonance is an exchange of energy between two things. It's a two-way experience, allowing each 'something' to come into balance with the other."

On the physical, mental, and emotional levels, we become like those around us because we are continually reinforcing patterns, behaviors, beliefs, and thoughts that have become the inherent culture and dynamic of that group or those relationships. Our minds will always filter out anything that doesn't serve the beliefs of that group and anything that doesn't match the resonance of that group won't even make it through to our conscious awareness.

So, when you're trying to do this deep, brave, life-changing work of healing your disorder in an environment that helped create it, it's going to be very difficult. I can feel the emotional charge of that sentence as I write it … I can feel the potential for resistance rising up within you and hear your possible thoughts: "What is she saying, that I need to end every relationship in my life in order to get healthy?" "Is she actually saying my family and friends made me bipolar?" or "Uh-huh, no way, I'm scared to step out of what I know, even though it may be a bit messed up sometimes – because at least I know what to expect and there's safety in that." And I get it, I hear you. And, I'm not telling you to do anything as drastic as separate yourself from your family and friends. At least not completely, and definitely not immediately.

What I am asking you to do is to bring awareness to who *you* are in those relationships and decide if that is the person you want to be and if those relationships can, in their current states, hold the space for you to become the healthy person you are in the process of becoming. You don't need to make any drastic changes or move a million miles away – although if that's what your inner whisper is telling you to do then explore that, be curious about it. Start creating some boundaries and testing them for fit. Try not to make any huge life changes until you've created a runway for yourself – and not until you've gotten your brain and body back into balance so that you know that that desire to make a big change is coming from your higher self and that it's something you can trust.

Until the day comes when you feel truly ready for big changes and you know that it's coming from your higher self, just focus on the little changes you can make today. This is the first step in finding and building your tribe.

Let that whisper tell you when you need to stay home instead of going to that birthday party or family gathering. Let it tell you when it's better to practice self-care instead of going out and celebrating. Let it tell you when you shouldn't pick up your phone, answer that text, or let yourself get dragged into some manufactured drama, but instead go take a walk or read a book. Even our healthy relationships or the people who have always supported us can create trigger points for us, so pay attention to when and how and with whom you get triggered. Then step back and thank your body for providing you with that guidance – because it's telling you that either, A) you have something inside of you that is ready to be healed and resolved or B) that person or situation is something that your guidance system is moving you away from. Or both. Either way, start looking at it as a gift and an opportunity to heal.

This phase in the healing process can be one of the very hardest because it has the potential to feel very lonely and isolating. Until you have created your new tribe, you may find yourself alone a lot. The ability to be alone with yourself but not feel lonely is a skill that is so helpful to build. So, bring awareness to that too and if you feel yourself dipping into a depressive episode because you're getting triggered by too much time alone, then reach out to someone. Do something that you know will bring some energy back to your system – this would be a good time to go take a fitness class or find a book reading or lecture that's happening on a subject that interests you or even go to a movie – at a theatre, by yourself – that you find funny or uplifting. Anything to shake you out of that cycle of feeling lonely, because that feeling, when left unchecked, can lead to desperation. And desperation can lead to you going against your guidance system and putting yourself back in an unhealthy situation, which can then trigger a full-blown episode and start the entire cycle all over again. This is another opportunity for you to bring compassion and gentleness to yourself. Keep telling yourself that this is the process of transformation, that you're safe, that you are not missing out but are choosing your health over everything else.

One word of caution here about support groups, because I actually don't recommend joining one as you go through this process. It might sound like a place to feel less alone and to find people who get you, but the truth is they usually aren't a place that fosters this type of full healing. Yes, sometimes, some of them can be amazing – but they can also be something that keeps you stuck, right where you're at, because the group is comprised of other people who are dealing with similar issues to yours – except they may not have the same intent as you do, which is to fully heal your disorder, illness or diagnosis. And intent is everything! Their intent might be to reinforce their belief of victimhood. They may not hold this new belief that you're creating for yourself that true healing is truly possible, they may want to blame society, or their genes, or their terrible life for their bipolar diagnosis. They might want to continue to use their diagnosis to justify harmful behavior. If this is the case but you are really feeling called to join a support group, then – find another group. Find one that is focused on healing, that has an energy of empowerment to it. This is the energy I create and foster in the groups I work with and it's the most beautiful thing to see my clients in full support to others in their healing circles. Just remember, trust yourself, let your emotions be your guide, and feel the energy of the room, then *listen* to the information your body is providing you, and, if it's an energy that doesn't feel good to you, or your body feels tension, tightness or constriction in any area, walk out!

I had to go through this phase too and had to make difficult choices to distance myself from my family and certain friends. There were several relationships that didn't make it – and that's okay. I honor and appreciate those people and relationships for what they were – and I understand that they needed to be released. My family is still my family and I love them very much – when push comes to shove, they will be there for me and I will be there for them. But, on a day-in, day-out basis I have had to create boundaries and skip out on family events. I also had to learn that my healing isn't always appreciated and this new version of me (this true version of me) can cause negative reactions in others. Because, it means that they may have to look at their own spaces that need healing and they are not always ready for that. So, I still get judged by some of my family members, I still get criticized and ostracized. But, it's happening less and less often and I now have members of my family who come to me for support and guidance. We are all just big mirrors for each other, so I know that I'm no longer being openly criticized because I have quieted my own inner critic and have come to a place of acceptance for myself.

As you begin to shift your current relationships, or move out of them altogether, you can also build new relationships with people that are aligned with your future self. This happened for me during my own healing. I had just recently become medication-free and started at the natural foods co-op. This was a whole new world for me and in that space, I didn't have to be the crazy one any longer. The new people that I met didn't know me as "Crazy Kate." Because they didn't see me as crazy, I could show up as the version of myself that I was fighting to become. It was at that point in my life, at that job, in that brand-new space, that the truth of me could be born. I felt like my true self was allowed to be seen for the very first time and

I was learning to trust myself and to create true self-love and acceptance. There were people that I met during this time that are still in my life today and are definitely a part of my tribe.

The things that we talked about in the last chapter on finding your joy will also lead you to your tribe. Your tribe is the group of people (or multiple groups of people) that really see you, that hold the same vision for your life that you hold for yourself, that believe in your healing, that honor your strengths and your weaknesses. They catch you when you fall and remind you to pick yourself back up and keep going. They make it safe for you to laugh at yourself because you know they're not judging. They walk alongside of you, but they don't feel the need to carry you or protect you or do it for you – because they believe in your own inherent ability to do these things for yourself. And you do all these things and hold all this space for them too. Your tribe is the living expression of true love. And when you find members of your tribe it's like finding yourself. It's like coming Home.

My tribe consists of people from all different areas of my life – they are members of my family, they are from the natural foods industry, from yoga, from my spiritual community, they are friends both old and new. I trust now that spark of recognition that happens in my system when I meet someone for the first time that is meant to be part of my tribe. I listen to that whisper when it speaks to me and I follow it by inviting that new person out for coffee, or to sit and have a conversation with me or even to take a trip with me. I put myself out there in sometimes uncomfortable ways, even though there's still that fear of rejection. Because I know that that spark that I'm feeling is my guidance and that my spirit is recognizing a friend.

I also want to honor how hard it is to put yourself out there when your go-to mode has been one of self-protection and preservation. It took me quite a while to get comfortable with this but, it is a skill that can be learned and strengthened over time. There was a time that I desperately wanted to start meeting new people; I joined about a million-different Meet Up groups and never went to a single one. I even went so far as to drive to a coffee shop where a book club that I had recently joined was meeting – and then sat in the parking lot, unable to go in, terrified and immobilized. After my panic attack subsided I drove home – feeling even worse about myself than I did before. This reinforced my belief that I'm not good enough, smart enough, or interesting enough and more firmly rooted it in my system. Don't do that – don't add insult to injury by berating yourself for being unable to take that next step. Be gentle with yourself (do I sound like a broken record yet?!), talk to yourself like you would your best friend. Tell yourself, as you sit in that parking lot, that you got one step closer this time. That next time you might even walk in the door. This disorder robs us of our sense of self, our confidence, and our feeling of belonging, so know that it may take time to put yourself out there.

When you do start to build your tribe, open up to all the new experiences that are possible. Your life is about to get a whole lot bigger and more beautiful. Each new person and every new experience creates a shift in how you see yourself and how you orient yourself in this new world that you're creating. Each new person and experience that you add will expand your capacity to actualize your own healing. These people and experiences will reinforce your new belief that you are meant to be fully-healed, that in fact, you are already healed. Your cells will change and align your body to being seen in this whole new way and your vibration will continue to rise to match the resonance of who and what's around you. You will know then that you have brought a deeper level of healing to yourself by spending more time with more people who see you as healthy and by expanding your mind, thoughts, beliefs, and preconceived notions through the exposure to many new people and experiences. And, as you continue to move through your healing journey you may find that your existing relationships, the ones that didn't fall away, have a new depth, connection and level of engagement. You may see that negative patterns are no longer present because you're no longer the same. You'll see that your relationships had to change in order to accommodate this new version of you. This is a beautiful process, so make sure to pause, acknowledge it and express gratitude for it. And give thanks to yourself for honoring your truth and being brave enough to show up in your relationships differently. This act of gratitude and acknowledgement will more firmly anchor in your new identity and will allow you to more clearly see the truth of who you are.

Chapter 10

Step 7 – Creating the Life That's Calling Out to You

"When you are inspired by some Great Purpose, some extraordinary project, all your thoughts break their bonds. Your mind transcends limitations, your consciousness expands in every direction, and you find yourself in a new, great and wonderful world. Dormant forces, faculties and talents become alive, and you discover yourself to be a greater person by far than you ever dreamed yourself to be."

– PATANJALI

Do you remember that belief system we talked about in Chapter 3? Here it is again if you need a refresher.

You have the power to fully heal yourself. You have everything needed to create a world for yourself where you are not mentally ill. You are meant to be healthy. True healing is truly possible and it's yours for the creating.

How are you doing with this? Is it beginning to resonate for you, even just a little bit? Can you feel your body starting to align to this belief? I hope so. If not, stay with it. Keep affirming it every day, multiple times through the day, first thing when you get up and right before you go to bed. Because it's having this belief firmly rooted in your system that is going to make all the other steps successful. Your intention and attention combine to create your reality and when you have those aligned and steering in the same direction, miracles can happen.

This was my starting point too and it was born out of a last-ditch attempt to save my life. I was giving myself one more shot to figure things out – and if I didn't find some relief, if I didn't get my bipolar under control, if I didn't start experiencing some peace and a bit of happiness, I was done. I would not be here today. I would have killed myself. So, I dug in and I told myself over and over again, until I started to believe myself, that I was going to find a way. This became my affirmation. This became my intention and the focal point of my attention.

As it turns out there's science to explain why having this belief firmly planted in my system is what created the opportunity for me to heal. I didn't know it at the time – I wasn't affirming healing for myself because of any knowledge of the Law of Attraction or quantum physics or epigenetics – I was just trying to save my life.

But, going back in time, I can see that I was teaching the cells in my body to align themselves around a state of healing and I was bringing my system into resonance with health by raising my vibration so that my body could inhabit the physical aspects of health.

In its simplest definition, Law of Attraction states that what you put your attention on is what will manifest in your life. Turns out that this definition is a huge simplification and that the truth of this universal law is way more intricate and involved. Not only do you need to put your focus on what it is you want, you also need to get yourself to a vibrational or energetic match of that thing you want – be it a new relationship, a new car, or a new state of health. Your body, mind, and heart need to be attuned to that new potential future, so much so that it already feels like truth to you – even before it's made real. Another thing to note here is that you are always working within the Law of Attraction – you are never exempt from it. You are either actively working to create the life you want by using the principles of this law or you are just letting your mind and body run on autopilot and live a life that will create more of the same experiences and stored emotions, so that they can continue to reinforce your old programming. Let's break it down so that you can not only understand it but, so you can use that knowledge to fully heal yourself – because, ultimately, taking the steps outlined in this book or any other book will not be enough if you don't also bring your entire system, mental, physical, emotional, and spiritual, into alignment.

Science, mainly neuroscience, is now able to prove what mystics have known for eons – and it's this, that we are beings that have capabilities within us to transform our lives and create a desired physical reality. We can do this by aligning our systems and focusing on our anticipated future state and by bringing your body into an energetic vibration that is a match for what you're trying to manifest. And, most importantly for someone with a mental illness, is that we are capable of transforming our bodies and healing ourselves. Here are the basic principles:

- All systems of the body are deeply connected. Nothing happens independently of the system itself. This is the reason this book focuses on whole-system healing and starts with the foundation of the physical body.
- The role of the mind is to create coherence between its conditioned programming and our physical reality. So, if you change your programming (conscious and subconscious mind) you can change your reality.
- Our genes can be taught or trained to function in new ways. We can change our genes and we are in charge of how our genes are regulated. Meaning – your body that is bipolar now does not need to be bipolar in the future.
- The very act of reaching for a thought that feels better (instead of holding onto a thought that feels bad) starts a physical process in the body that creates and connects new neurons/neuropeptides in your brain and in your heart and begins to align your entire body to this better feeling thought or new way of being.
- Illness and disease are just our body's ways of trying to effectively move out traumas and bring our attention to behaviors, thoughts, and beliefs that are no longer

serving us. Traditional talk therapy can only take you so far, for two reasons: 1) the body has its own memory of those traumas and needs the opportunity to process, heal, and release them. 2) it focuses almost entirely on looking back versus actively changing outdated thoughts, beliefs, and behaviors and developing the skillset to fully heal and create the life you want.

- Our power comes from consciously choosing our thoughts as well as how we respond to the emotions that arise in our bodies. Remember, we are not our emotions and we are not our thoughts. Our thoughts are a side-effect of the lives we lived, the experiences we've had, and the beliefs that have been programmed into us. We get to choose which thoughts to listen to and give the most attention to and how to respond to them. And our emotions are meant to move through us and act as a navigational system. We are not meant to take them on as our truth and anchor them into the body.
- We are, at a structural level, more energy than matter. And, the majority of the information carried throughout our bodies is not via our physical system – it's carried and communicated via electrical and magnetic systems – our own energetic field. Therefore, when you change your energy, you change your life.
- We cannot effectively heal until we align all the systems of our body to the belief of health and the state of health; when we do this, we put ourselves in alignment with that future healthy state and are connected to the quantum field – the space where every possibility exists,

including the one where your bipolar disorder is fully healed.

- Our job then is to shift our focus from the physical (our disorder and all the ways that it's running our lives) to the energy of health, the feeling of health, the belief of health, and the field where healing exists.
- Your power to heal will come when you combine the power of your mind with the power of your body. Here's how:
  - Create coherence in your mind (meaning get clear on what your intention is). I mean like crystal clear – define it, visualize it, describe who you are in that space and what your life looks like when you are fully healed. This coherence will then manifest a possibility in the quantum field for this future reality to become physically true for you.
  - Then, create coherence in your heart (meaning, how do you feel when you are no longer bipolar, when your disorder has been healed?). Literally feel these feelings in your body. Let your imagination go to the place where that future reality feels real and let your body feel what that new state of being feels like. Then bring in the feelings of gratitude, feel grateful for healing, for that state of true health, knowing that it's coming, that you're creating it. Feel gratitude so deeply and completely, to the point where your system believes that that future reality is already here. Today. Now.

- And from this coherent state, your desired outcome will be able to manifest fully in your life. When you combine this process of visualization with right thinking and right action (Steps 1-6 in this book) you become the conscious, deliberate, powerful creator of your life. Your disorder no longer runs the show. You do. And this is how the Universe delivers your miracle – except that now you know it's not really a miracle, it's the full divinity and power that is you.

This is the Law of Attraction in Action!

Here's the process I recommend for bringing your brain and body into coherence around this future state of health. It's the process that I've used for years to create all sorts of desired outcomes, not just healing my bipolar. It continues to evolve as I acquire new information – but it's always a version of this:

- Spend some time, a few days, a weekend or the course of a month to get clear on your desired outcome. Take the time you need, that feels right in your body and that allows you the space to fully explore and imagine what you want your life to look like. Is it fully healing your bipolar disorder? Is it getting your current diagnosis to a manageable state? Is it extending your healing out to include not just your disorder but possible other health issues you're facing? Does it include freeing yourself from your traumas? Is it never having a panic attack again? Is it being medication-free? Define, very clearly, what this future looks like to you.

- Who are you once you are in that future state? What does your body look like? How does your body feel? What practices have you implemented that brought you to this state of healing? What emotional wounds have you healed and released? What's your energy level like? What new activities have you incorporated into your life? What's in your life that brings you a sense of joy and purpose? How does your life look different? Do you act differently? Talk differently? Are you in a new job? What's happening with your relationships? Who are the people around you? What does your tribe look like?
- Get really clear and specific on the details and capture them, either by doing an audio recording of what you're visualizing or writing it down.

- Then decide how you want to feel in this desired state. Let your body really feel this imagined future – see what emotions come up for you, what resonates in your body. Define them and capture them with your intention. If it's too hard to go to the positive feelings right off the bat you can define the feeling you no longer want to feel, then identify its opposite as your new, desired feeling. Your body needs the opportunity to feel this future state – so let yourself go wild with this. Use your imagination in a way you haven't in years so that that imagined reality feels real in your body. Here are some positive feeling words to get the brainstorm session flowing:

- o Accepted, Alive, Appreciated, Authentic, Balanced, Blessed, Boundless, Brave, Calm, Capable, Centered, Clear, Confident, Connected, Courageous, Creative, Curious, Determined, Elated, Embodied Empowered, Energized, Engaged, Focused, Free, Generous, Grateful, Grounded, Guided, Happy, Healed, Hopeful, Impassioned, Important, Innovative, Inspired, Joyful, Liberated, Love/Loving/Loved, Nurtured, Optimistic, Passionate, Peaceful, Playful, Powerful, Prosperous, Refreshed, Relaxed, Sacred, Safe, Secure, Seen, Strong, Supported/Supportive, Unified, Valued, Vibrant, Whole

These first two steps are putting right thought with right feeling and aligning your mind and heart to this future that you're creating.

- Once you're clear on what your life looks and feels like in this new state, then create a visual representation of it. There are lots of options here – you can make a vision board, create a scrapbook, make a Mind Movie – or do what I do and use a PowerPoint. It's a medium that I'm comfortable with because I use it regularly in my job and I'm a paperless kind of girl, so I like having it on my computer for mobility and ease of use. Find images that represent what that future state LOOKS like and FEELS like to you. You want to capture both the physical reality and the emotionality of it. Find images that make you connect to that future reality and that allow you to feel those emotions. Have fun with this process. Let your inner-child come out and be a part of this creation. You can grab pictures from magazines, print them off your computer doing Google image searches or if you want to get really creative you can draw or paint your desired outcome.

- The next step is to write an affirmation about it and add that affirmation to your visual medium. The affirmation should be written from the present tense (meaning, I AM statements instead of I WILL BE statements). Your affirmation could go something like this:
    - I am completely healthy. The bipolar disorder that I suffered from for years is totally healed. And I am now living my life medication-free. My body feels energized and in balance. I have repaired the relationships that needed repairing and released the ones that no longer served me. My relationships are now all healthy and supportive. I now feel safe in my body and know that it is my partner on this journey. I spend time in gratitude and joy every day – knowing that my life is my own. My world is expanding through many new experiences and I feel a sense of excitement for the life that I'm building for myself. I know that I can trust myself and that my Soul is always leading me toward a life that is filled with love, meaning, gratitude, passion, and play.

- The final step is that you need to use this powerful tool that you just created. Spend time with it every day. You need to spend so much time with it that it begins to feel more real to you than your current physical life does. Spend so much time with it that the excitement bubbles over into your entire life. And, know that it's not going to feel like that at first. When you initially start working with this there is going to be a voice in your head that is saying, 'Yeah right, as if. You're fooling yourself. This is all a load of crap. It can't possibly be this easy.' But stay with it, do it anyway. And by that, I mean, commit to a daily practice. For me, I do this in the morning right before meditation. That way I get to take my intentions and my amazing feeling state into my meditation practice, quiet my mind, and let myself connect on a vibrational level to that future outcome. I know now, after having had this practice work in my life time after time, that my desire is just waiting for me to come into a state of coherence so that it can show up fully in my life. I will typically spend 15–30 minutes in my visioning process (it depends on how many intentions I'm working with at any given time). I repeat my affirmations out loud because the physical vibration created by using my voice supports the energetic vibration. And then I move into a 20–30-minute meditation, invite the wholeness of me to come fully present, and then allow my brain and body to quiet so that all my systems can come into coherence and meet the vibrational energy of my intentions. This is a process I work closely on with my clients. I hold them accountable to doing this visioning work daily because I see, repeatedly, the impact that it has.

This process is sort of ridiculously simple, but don't let its simplicity make you think that it isn't incredibly powerful. There are three other things to note with this process.

The first is that you have to combine this with right action. That means act as if you're already healthy. Identify how that healthy version of you would act, then act like that. This is why this book isn't just all about positive affirmations and raising your vibration – it starts with healing the physical chemistry of the body and walks you through steps you can take that will support your body in releasing trauma and getting online with this new way of being.

Second, it will only work if you work it (just like recovery programs teach). It needs to be a top priority, *the* top priority of your life – because you are literally saving your life and creating one that feels amazing to you. So, commit to yourself by committing to this practice. Spend time with it every single day.

And, third, the Universe, or Field, has a way of bringing our intentions to us in ways that are unexpected – and this is a good thing because if it's something you fully expect, your brain will be able to talk you out of the fact that you created this miracle for yourself. It will be able to jam it into its preconditioned programming and tell you that it was a fluke or run of the mill. So, hold the intention but allow the HOW of it to show up for you in magical and unexpected ways. What this might look like in relation to healing bipolar disorder is that you could be thinking that you must go searching for a doctor to help you with your medication withdrawal process – and you even make an appointment with someone you find online but aren't totally sure is the right fit. But the day before your appointment you meet a naturopath at a class you were in and feel a slight uptick in your energy. Recognize this as the possible opportunity it is – the Universe delivering to you the perfect person to support you in your healing process. Then give yourself permission to course correct and cancel your existing appointment so that you can work with the perfect person that you manifested for yourself. And when these things show up, these synchronicities, thank the Universe and ask for more.

How are you doing? Are you still with me? It's okay if you're feeling overwhelmed or intimidated or skeptical. If I hadn't already lived through this and witnessed the healing in others, I would be too. So, if you need to, step away. Take some time for this to settle into your brain and body. And know that you have a choice to make. Reading this book may be challenging your belief systems, it may be triggering you in all kinds of ways. But you have the power to choose. You can choose to stay firmly rooted in your current belief system, the one that created your bipolar disorder, or you can choose a new outcome, the one that will free you from your limitations. I am holding the space for you to choose the latter. I know that healing is possible – I am no more special or different than you. So make the choice and continue making it every day.

Chapter 11

Yes, This Work Is Hard... But Do It Anyway

"The human spirit is as expansive as the cosmos. This is why it is so tragic to belittle yourself or to question your worth. No matter what happens continue to push back the boundaries of your inner life. The confidence to prevail over any problem, the strength to overcome adversity and unbounded hope – all reside within you."

– Daisaku Ideda

You were led to this book for a reason. Your Soul, Higher Self, Inner Guide is whispering to you. There is a part of you that already knows that healing is possible and your system was crying out for a way to make it happen. So, you are here for a reason. Everything that has happened in your life has brought you to this point. And you can't unlearn something, you can't unread this book. Which means that now, you get to make the choice of what to do with it.

This ability to choose is incredibly powerful. And your system is already starting to reorganize itself around the possibility of full and complete healing. You will just need to stick with it – and this, my dear friend, is where the real work begins. It is not enough for you to just read this and talk about the concepts and incorporate a few of the teachings. You need to do the work that will put your entire system in a state of health.

If you go down this path you will be fighting the programming of your mind – and 95% of our time is spent operating from the subconscious programming and 70% of that subconscious programming is negative. So, it's going to take dedication and effort to reprogram your mind and choose thoughts, behaviors, and beliefs that support your new way of being.

You are going to be working against the current state of your body, which has become conditioned to the drama created from your current way of living. Your body has become addicted to the hormones going through it that are caused by the stresses you're under, the food you eat, and your lack of sleep and the constant yo-yo of your emotions.

You will also be battling the commonly-held beliefs of your family, your doctors, and society in general. You will find that, surprisingly enough (or at least, it surprised me), very few people will understand or support this journey that you're embarking on. It could be because they're frightened for you. It could be because it's bumping up against their own negative programming. It could be because they're unhealthy themselves and they want you to remain in that space with them. Whatever their reasons you may find yourself doing this with almost no support.

If you choose to go down this path you are going to have to take full responsibility for everything in your life. That doesn't mean that you are to blame (although in certain situations you may need to own your part in creating those painful experiences) but it does mean that nothing in your life exists without you having played a part in creating it. And if you've actively hurt someone or something you are going to have face that shame, head on. And blast it with as much love and compassion as you can muster. You must turn around and look in the mirror and face your fears, pains, and past. All of it. And to me, this is both the most gruesome and most beautiful process in the world. To those of you doing it I bow to you because it's infinitely hard. But … oh, so, worth, it.

If you keep going on this path you're going to have to release things that no longer fit. This could be anything from your favorite food to your best friend and everything in between.

And if you keep going still, you'll be guided to try new things, get uncomfortable, and expose yourself to possible rejection. You're going to have to get good with failure – because you will not succeed at every new endeavor you set out on and not everything you try will end up feeling good to you.

Probably hardest of all, if you choose to follow this path you are going to have to once and for all face those spaces in you where your unworthiness lies. Where you hold your pain. Where you hold the belief that you're inherently unlovable. Take a big, deep breath and just be with that one for a moment.

You will do all this knowing that it's a process that is going to take time. You will not be able to unravel all those deep dark places inside yourself, change your programming, and elevate your habits immediately. You are bound to get frustrated, to want to give up, to want to go back to what feels familiar. You may even start to question if it's all worth it and if your bipolar disorder was any worse than this.

And – the truth is that it may not be (although I'm willing to debate you on this). But what is equally true is that what is on the other side of this work is a million times better than living with bipolar disorder. What's on the other side of this work is a world where mental illness no longer exists. And the process of transformation oftentimes is itself painful and messy and terrifying but it is always worth it. Because you emerge stronger, braver, and wiser. You are more capable of giving and receiving love. You are intimately more connected to yourself. You are now able to bring compassion and empathy to others who are suffering. You can now show up fully in your own life. Empowered. Energized and more alive than you ever knew was possible. And you can use that newfound energy to create a life that is filled with all the things that, up to this point, you have only been able to dream of.

My fervent hope for you is that you choose to continue. That you choose to follow your own path of healing and let it burn away everything that is no longer true for you. And that you emerge as your whole, divine self. Because it's radiantly beautiful.

"I am not what happened to me, I am what I choose to become."

– C.G. Jung

Chapter 12

Honor What Was and Make Space for What Is Becoming

"Special love today to anyone who is finally on the rise. May every step of your journey be blessed, and may you be braver than you ever knew you could be. But most of all, may you offer limitless patience to yourself along the way. Changing your life is hard, and – like all hard things – it requires love and endurance. But you are worthy, and you are strong, and you can do this."

– Elizabeth Gilbert

Your healing journey will ultimately be different than mine – because we are different. We have different life experiences, different relationships, different belief systems, different fears, different truths, different programs, different bodies. But we are also the same. Our spirits come from the same Universal Source and we are both here to fully inhabit this experience of living.

We have the same divine gifts – the ability to create and to heal. So, when I say that true healing is truly possible and it's yours for the creating, I am speaking truth. Because this is what I did for myself and what I've helped my clients do for themselves. And your ability to create a miracle in your own life is the same as my ability is to create one in mine.

I've given you the steps that have worked for me and have provided lots of options for you to experiment with. Below is a list of things that I suggest you build your foundation on, then incorporate other modalities as you're able or as you feel called to.

1. 30-day elimination diet using the Whole 30 method; make sure to cut out all sugar, dairy, gluten, food dyes, factory farmed meat and eggs, highly processed oils, and alcohol. Eat only whole foods and lots of dark, leafy greens. Buy organic if your budget allows and whenever possible.
2. Supplement with probiotics, a food-based multivitamin and mineral, omega 3s, vitamin D, a B complex, and magnesium.
3. Create a sleep routine.
4. Meditate – daily.
5. Exercise – mindfully and with purpose, at least 3 days per week.
6. Find a somatic practitioner to help you with trauma release. Work with other healers or try other methods that you're curious about.

7. Bring awareness to your thoughts and emotions; begin to separate yourself from them so you stop identifying as them.
8. Follow your curiosities.
9. Build a tribe – if you have someone in your life that you know can support you on your journey then enlist their help, have them read this book, use them as your accountability partner.
10. Create a vision for your healing and your future self – then spend time with it every day.

These steps will create the infrastructure for complete healing. Together, they encompass your total system, including your physical, mental, emotional, and spiritual bodies. Incorporate additional modalities from this book or try other ones that you are curious about. Let your body guide you – it will tell you which ones to use and which to save for later or forgo altogether.

Start taking radical responsibility for your own healing. Stop putting it in the hands of your doctor or your therapist. Stop giving your power away to your mom or your spouse. Only you can do this work for you. No one else in your life needs to change, show up differently, or walk this path with you. I'm going to say that again because it's a biggie: no one in your life needs to do anything different than what they've been doing and what they're doing right now in order for you to begin your healing journey and to stay on it. This is your journey. Own it fully. Remember that you're a powerful being and you have everything you need inside of you already to do this work – if you didn't you wouldn't be reading this book.

An important thing to keep in mind as you do this work is that you are going to bump up against your own resistance time and time again – and more often than not it will be your fear of success, not your fear of failure, that will end up holding you back and keeping you stuck in a place of disease. Fully committing to this path *is* going to change the course of your life forever. You will no longer able to play small, be a victim, or hide your mistakes behind a veil of your mental illness. You will be called to show up fully as the star of your own life. The Universe is going to nudge you every once and awhile with a perceived challenge or set back to see if you're really committed, if you're serious about this work. Keep answering YES. Your mind is going to protect its programming by trying to keep you from moving forward – don't listen to it.

Because –

- You are worthy.
- You are not broken.
- You – as you exist today – not having done this work yet – are unconditionally loved and are capable of giving and receiving that love.
- Everything you've done or experienced up until this point is exactly what it needed to be – and you can now choose a different way.
- You belong on this planet, in your body, fully living your life. You are not here by mistake.
- You are doing brave work and I applaud you.

I know the horrors that are bipolar disorder. You no longer need to exist in that space. You can choose to heal. And I also know the beauty of bipolar – please don't fear the loss of energy, creativity or passion that shows up for you during a manic episode. These feelings are so much closer to your true state of being than the feelings that arise during a depressive episode. You're not going to lose them. When these energizing feelings arise in a body that's balanced and healthy, they don't overpower. They enhance. You will be able to let them express fully without the fear of losing control. You will be able to use them to create infinite magic and meaning in your life.

So, as you make your choice to fully step into your healing process, know that I am here, holding the space for you, believing in you, your strength, wisdom, and divine right to live a life that feels authentically yours.

Remember that your first and most important step is to build your belief system around this truth – that you are meant to be healthy and that real, lasting healing is yours for the creating.

"Be who you were created to be and you will set the world on fire."

– St. Catherine of Sienna

About the Author

Kate LaBrosse is a best-selling author and motivational speaker who trained with Presence-Based® Coaching for her ICF certification. She is an expert in the natural products industry and has worked as a Wellness Buyer for a national retailer, as a National Sales Manager for a probiotic brand, and most recently as the National Director of Conventional for a sales and marketing company.

Kate has been on a personal journey of healing and transformation for most of her life. Her history includes family addiction, parental abandonment, sexual abuse, rape, and multiple suicide attempts. She was diagnosed with anxiety, depression, and ultimately bipolar II disorder in her mid-twenties. After years of battling her disorder with conventional medications and therapy, she eventually healed her mental illness and childhood traumas naturally using a whole-system approach, combining healing modalities that support the mental, physical, emotional, and spiritual bodies, and has been medication- and symptom-free for almost ten years.

Kate uses her spiritual gifts – which include the ability to channel energy and information, expertise in the natural products industry, and knowledge gained from her own healing – to support others who are ready to take back their power and embark on their own journeys of healing and transformation.

Thank You!

Thank you for reading This Is Me, Bipolar-Free! I sincerely hope that my story and book have provided a roadmap for your healing journey and opened the space within you to believe in your own ability to heal your mental illness. If you're feeling that possibility alive within you and want support on your journey, head on over to my website, www.katelabrosse.com, to get a free toolkit that will jumpstart your healing process.

The fact that you've gotten this far in the book tells me one very important thing about you: that your inner whisper is telling you that you're ready to truly heal and create a fully-lived, authentic life! So, if you're feeling called to fully commit to your own healing and want to schedule a strategy session with me, let's do it! Go to www.katelabrosse.com/strategysession to request a time to talk with me. Until then, know that I'm sending you love and light and already see you as healed, whole, and living your best life!

xoxo

Kate

Printed in the USA
CPSIA information can be obtained
at www.ICGtesting.com
JSHW082346140824
68134JS00020B/1903

9 781642 794229